C++ Programming

Good Principles
For
Excellent Endings

Edition Zero

C++ Programming: Good Principles For Excellent Endings

ISBN: 978-1-4466-6245-8

Copyright © 2011 Onda Technology

Copyright © 2011 João Paredes

All rights reserved.

Credits

Contents: João Paredes

Cover design: Bruno Santos
              João Paredes

By **Onda Media** & **pluie/noir**

Important warning

Welcome to the Edition Zero of this book. This is part of Onda Technology's internal collection of teaching materials. It was decided to release this non-reviewed version to test community acceptance and to gather input on the quality of the book. Therefore, it was given the tag "Edition Zero". It is a pre-release version, without the final appendices like the Index, Glossary or the Bibliography. So, don't expect the quality of the final product in this release. Our hopes are that we can gather comments from early adopters that allow us to improve this manual, so that a premium quality First Edition can be made available. Later, we will be selecting, among the contributors, a few that will be offered the final version of the First Edition, before anyone else is even allowed to buy it. For eligibility and more information about our projects, you should check out our website at

```
http://www.ondatechnology.org/
```

We also kindly ask that you consider donating to support our projects.

For my quintessential random number

Special thanks to:

My Father, for helping with the review process

My friend Bruno Santos, for the beautiful cover design

And the lovely Sara, for all the patience during the final stages of this project

Table of Contents

    Credits..3
Table of Contents..11
1 Introduction..17
2 Your project..23
    2.1 Organizing your project...............................24
    2.2 Project management tools............................28
        2.2.1 Code Editors and IDEs........................29
        2.2.2 Version management............................32
        2.2.3 Project construction.............................35

- 2.3 Project documentation..38
  - 2.3.1 Types of documentation.......................................38
    - 2.3.1.1 Product specification...................................38
    - 2.3.1.2 High Level Architecture..............................39
    - 2.3.1.3 Low Level Architecture...............................40
    - 2.3.1.4 Application Programming Interface...............40
    - 2.3.1.5 Product manual....................................41
    - 2.3.1.6 Online help..42
    - 2.3.1.7 Safety warnings....................................43
  - 2.3.2 Helper tools..44
    - 2.3.2.1 Doxygen..44
    - 2.3.2.2 Wikis..45
    - 2.3.2.3 Visio, Dia...45
- 2.4 Deploying your project..45
  - 2.4.1 Deployment policy and licensing........................46
  - 2.4.2 Deployment methods..47
    - 2.4.2.1 Binary versus source...............................47
    - 2.4.2.2 Hard copies versus network........................48
- 2.5 The team..49
  - 2.5.1 Interaction..49
  - 2.5.2 Communication..50
  - 2.5.3 Hiring..53
    - 2.5.3.1 Pressure factors...................................54
    - 2.5.3.2 Learn to read them.................................56
    - 2.5.3.3 Evaluate the dynamic response....................59
- 3 Code organization..63
- 3.1 Code formatting style..64
  - 3.1.1 Alignment..64
  - 3.1.2 Spaces...66
  - 3.1.3 Brackets...67

3.2 Header files logic..68
3.3 File layout..70
3.4 Naming conventions..78
3.5 Mixing C and C++..80
    3.5.1 Compiler requirements..81
    3.5.2 Code specifics...81
4 Defensive programming..85
4.1 Code reuse..86
4.2 Preprocessor..87
    4.2.1 Conditional compilation...88
        4.2.1.1 Portability and feature selection...................88
        4.2.1.2 Preprocessor assisted debugging..................92
        4.2.1.3 Macros..95
    4.2.2 Compilation process debugging............................97
    4.2.3 Obsolescence...98
4.3 Variables...100
    4.3.1 Comparisons and assignments............................100
    4.3.2 Variable misuse..104
    4.3.3 Pointer arithmetic problems................................105
    4.3.4 String constants...105
    4.3.5 Casts...106
4.4 Compiler messages...107
    4.4.1 Errors..108
        4.4.1.1 Undeclared identifier...................................108
        4.4.1.2 Functions are abstract.................................108
        4.4.1.3 Undefined reference....................................109
        4.4.1.4 Undefined reference to 'main'......................109
    4.4.2 Warnings..110
        4.4.2.1 Comparison between signed and unsigned..110
        4.4.2.2 Member initializers will be reordered..........110
        4.4.2.3 Suggest parenthesis around assignment.......111

4.4.3 Special case: function warnings............................111
4.5 Memory management..112
    4.5.1 Allocation..113
    4.5.2 Leaks..115
    4.5.3 Cleanup...116
    4.5.4 Suicidal objects..117
    4.5.5 Placement new..118
4.6 User input..119
4.7 Functions...121
    4.7.1 Error handling..122
    4.7.2 Inline functions and methods.............................124
    4.7.3 Variable arguments...127
    4.7.4 Returning from a function.................................131
    4.7.5 Function overloading caveats............................132
    4.7.6 Notable functions..134
        4.7.6.1 The gets function.......................................134
        4.7.6.2 The *printf family of functions..................135
4.8 Managing temporary storage......................................136
5 Classes and objects..141
5.1 Your API..142
    5.1.1 Good Ideas..142
        5.1.1.1 Organize your global namespace................142
        5.1.1.2 Proper interfaces...142
5.2 Constructors and destructors......................................142
    5.2.1 Bad ideas...143
        5.2.1.1 Chaining constructors.................................143
        5.2.1.2 Using exceptions in destructors..................143
        5.2.1.3 Explicitly calling a destructor on a local.....144
        5.2.1.4 Calling virtual functions.............................144
        5.2.1.5 Relying in the order of static initialization. .147

5.2.1.6 Unnecessary default constructors................150
5.2.2 Good ideas...150
　5.2.2.1 Using initialization lists................................150
　5.2.2.2 Using "this" inside the constructor..............151
　5.2.2.3 Using exceptions in constructors.................151
　5.2.2.4 Dynamic memory? Copy constructor..........152
5.3 Inheritance specifics...153
　5.3.1 Bad ideas...154
　　5.3.1.1 Changing member visibility........................154
　　5.3.1.2 Being too literal with notions in classes......154
　5.3.2 Good ideas..155
　　5.3.2.1 Virtual constructors......................................155
　　5.3.2.2 Virtual destructors..155
　　5.3.2.3 Protecting derived classes from breaking....156
　　5.3.2.4 Using abstract classes and interfaces...........156
　　5.3.2.5 Having private virtuals.................................157
5.4 Exceptions...157
5.5 Friends..160
5.6 Operator overloading..160
　5.6.1 Good ideas..161
　　5.6.1.1 Keeping the semantics.................................161
　　5.6.1.2 Protecting your assignment operators..........162
　　5.6.1.3 Using prefix operators..................................163
　　5.6.1.4 Dynamic memory? Assignment overload....164
5.7 Binary trees safety..164
6 Optimizations..171
6.1 Explicit Major Optimizations......................................173
　6.1.1 Caching...174
　6.1.2 Buffering...175
　6.1.3 Lazy evaluation and pro-activity........................176
　6.1.4 Data structure optimizations...............................177

      6.1.4.1 Linked lists..177
      6.1.4.2 Matrix abstraction classes...........................180
  6.2 Detail optimizations...181
    6.2.1 Data based optimizations....................................181
      6.2.1.1 Data bundling..181
      6.2.1.2 Data alignment..182
      6.2.1.3 Data packing..182
      6.2.1.4 Common subexpression elimination............184
      6.2.1.5 Constant propagation..................................185
    6.2.2 Loop Optimizations..185
      6.2.2.1 Array Iterations...186
      6.2.2.2 Loop invariant code motion........................187
      6.2.2.3 Loop interchange...189
      6.2.2.4 Loop fusion...191
      6.2.2.5 Loop fission...192
      6.2.2.6 Loop reversal...193
      6.2.2.7 Loop unrolling..195
      6.2.2.8 Loop unswitching..197
7 Final notes...199

1 Introduction

The first thing one must have in mind, when starting a project, is that developing software is not just writing code. It is a very complex process with many stages, layers and tools. Therefore, good programming practices are not just writing good code, they extend a long way beyond that. Creating software also includes writing both user and developer documentation, writing comments, debugging, creating project files, managing versions, designing an interface and team work. It is important to maintain good policies in all of those stages. You need to properly format your code, write comments that are easy to understand, use the right methodologies to debug your project, respect your team mates and have in place the appropriate communication means to coordinate work with them, write simple yet sophisticated and extensible project files and provide the desired feedback to your end user because good code is useless without a properly designed interface.

A lot in this book is oriented towards defensive programming. The world would be a better place if everyone applied these principles to their projects. For a start, a lot less people would be on drugs due to the frustration of losing entire hours or days worth of work due to a software crash. Defensive programming is not just about code, it's about the whole process of developing software, from the simple initial planning steps, up to the time you're about to distribute the product. Programming is not only a science, it also introduces some art. Because there are many ways to achieve a specific result, the programmer feels the pressure of the need to choose one that he thinks is appropriate and, more importantly, every bit of code he writes gets a little of his experience and his life in it. Mastering the ability to write good code and choosing the right paths is something that can take a very long time.

You see, computers are, basically, dumb. They do exactly what you tell them to do. However, they do not guess what you want them to do. The trick is to learn how to tell them what you want. Bugs, fatal exceptions, blue screens, kernel panics, and the like, aside from hardware failures for various reasons, they all come down to the inconvenient truth that you, or someone else, failed to tell them what was expected from them. Somewhere, along the line, someone gave an incorrect statement, entered incorrect data, or ambiguities were left dangling in the code. Even if it is not in your own code, such failure to issue the proper orders is a human error, even if it is someone else's. The same way "guns don't kill people, people do", "computers don't make mistakes, people do".

So, this manual is as an introduction or a collection of pointers and tips on how you can improve your practice. It is intended for people who have already some knowledge about programming in C and C++, but are not yet experienced in the development of big projects. It will most likely be very helpful for students and other people with a more academic rather than professional experience.

One company I worked for had the type of business that required quality on its products above what is considered to be commercially typical. It developed a very special kind of machines. Software for those machines really had to be of top of the line quality. Otherwise, a lot of money might be lost. I was hired as R&D manager and was put in charge of hiring the remainder of the team for a new division to be setup in my country. When I arrived at that position, software development was done in a division placed in another country, there were no project management techniques or policies in place, team coordination was centralized to a single man that delegated no management tasks, and their concept of code management was dumping it on a network share that the manager would add to its own personal version control system to which no one else had access. Also, the quality of the team members left much to be desired, from the code I was able to inspect. There was also no documentation and yet they expected to pass the certification process from the most hard to convince certification entities in the world. Two months after my arrival, the company had a brand new state-of-the art division with proper development policies, including adequate source code and documentation management infrastructures and, more than that, a well trained and united team that, in that time, was not only able to understand the poor quality legacy code the company had, but also fix a lot of the problems it had, despite being a fraction of the size of the previous team.

As you will be able to see, it's not only good code that makes a good program. It is also a good planning, a good team, good communication and good leadership. And the problems of bad software really do show. Between some problems that just add to our frustration and others that are critical, fatalities have occurred, more than once, due to software problems. One such example was with a piece of medical equipment, a CT scan machine, the Therac-25, which, due to a race condition occurring in the software, resulted in the unfortunate event of a few patients receiving a lethal dose of radiation.

Computers have evolved a lot, as did software. And it is inevitable that they will keep evolving. Change is inevitable. However, the conformism of some, bad decisions of others, and the exaggerated optimism and reliance in legacy systems, has brought us some ties that prevent us from taking the full power of what current computing technologies can offer. It is no mystery that the amount of effort put into devising means to keep some backwards compatibility seriously hampers the efficiency of our systems. Don't get me wrong, I'm not trying to bash the scientists and engineers that brought us to our current state of technological evolution. Many of them were doing their best with what they had, others were just following orders and, at that time, they were also in the beginning and learning, alone, what we, today, take for granted from any computer science course or properly chosen set of books. Rules and guidelines that, today, help us produce good software, were still to be written at some point in the past, when they were first needed. And this is not a symptom unique to computer engineering. So, it is up to you to try to do your best with your tools, and avoid wasting the resources you have today.

Throughout this text, you'll be reading a lot of advices, recommending you to do some of the things using some specific method or advising you to avoid some other method. This does not mean, however, that you should always do exactly as described. In some situations you'll find yourself using some other legacy framework that does things in a different manner, possibly in some way you've been advised not to, or you'll come to the conclusion that there is no other way besides doing exactly the opposite of what you read. If that happens, it does not mean that you are not a good programmer or that your project is poorly planned. Sometimes you have really no other way. You just need to learn how to distinguish such situations from bad software engineering.

2 Your project

Today we are lucky enough to have at our disposal several tools to aid us in building projects. If a project is no more than one source file, some of the tools become either irrelevant or overkill. However, such projects are nowadays rare and are usually no more than short programs you write to either test something (like, for instance, a specific library or library feature) or to demonstrate something. This makes it important to properly know the tools available so you can enhance the productivity to your full potential. You also need to understand that a product is never finished. Besides being subject to several iterations during development, even after you introduce it to the market, you will still have to provide support, which will include the need to perform bug corrections and deploy updates and new features.

2.1 Organizing your project

Software can be (and usually is) a quite complex project with a few layers. On the top, we have the presentation layer. The presentation layer is the interface with which your product communicates with its end user. It can be a graphical user interface, a command line interface or, in the case of your product being a library or a driver, instead of having an interactive interface to the end user, provide an API[1] which other programs, or the operating system, use to talk to your product. You need to develop the presentation layer – or interface – of the program in such a way that it can efficiently interact with either the final user or other software, depending on what the project is. It needs to be carefully planned and designed to be aware and resilient to being provided with incorrect input and to provide appropriate and understandable output. There are many cases of companies able to create software with a very high level of quality of code, but with interfaces that leave much to be desired by being both confusing and unfriendly to the user. Be aware that being user friendly does not imply having pretty colors or good looking icons. Designing an interface is much harder than it looks at

---

1 *Application Programming Interface is a set of classes, function calls, macros, variables and values that a software product uses to interact with another software product.*

first glance because it implies that the interface designer needs to have in mind the aspects of the functionality such interface has to provide and a way to present that functionality in an organized, intuitive and properly documented fashion.

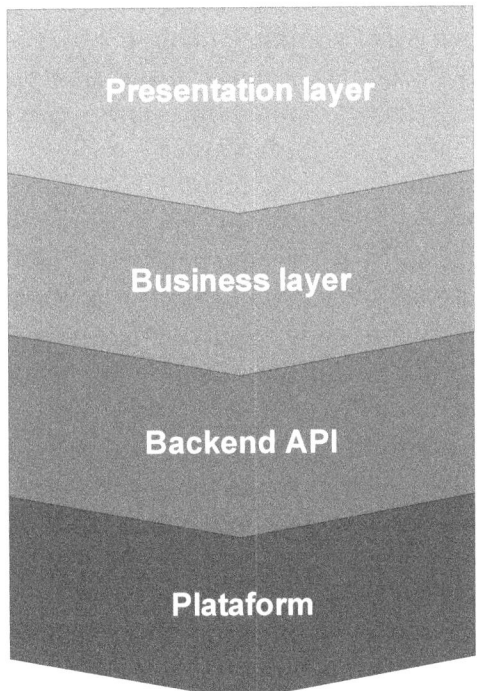

Image 1: Layers of a software product

Then, there is the Business Layer. The business layer is the layer where all the major processing of the product is done. It is, basically, the heart, the brain, the engine of your product. Whatever functions, features, functionalities and processing that your product has to supply or perform, that are specific to its purpose, can be found in that layer. Although the business layer is mostly code, there are several other components of it. Reference documentation and comments on the code are equally as important. Even if you are the only one to maintain such code, you'll need to keep track of how that layer has to work, what's been done, what is supposed to be done, how it was done and what's missing. **Don't you ever, even for a second, think that you're infallible and that later you'll be able to remember what you did.** Assumption is the mother of all things you'll regret. Marking things as yet unfinished by using comments is a good idea. Define a keyword, "`TODO`" for example. Then it is possible to find out easily what's still missing. You can "`grep`" your way out. If you're not familiar with the "`grep`" tool, become familiar. It allows to search a file or a set of files for a specific regular expression pattern. In this case, you can just search for "`TODO`" and obtain a list of unfinished items. The same effect can be obtained from the "Find in Files" option of your IDE.

> Take notes, use "TODO" comments in your code.

Under the business layer, we have the Backend API and the Platform. The backend API is an API developed to help hide the specific details of the platform from the business layer. The Platform is both the operating system and hardware on which your software runs and the specific implementation layer you built to adapt your software to that set, hidden from your business layer by the backend API. The objective is to have the business layer as independent as possible from the platform. This will not only allow the possibility of easily porting the program to other platforms, but will also help maintain and keep the software up to date, should the platforms on which it runs evolve. In any case, you will only have to make minor corrections to the implementation under the backend API while keeping your Business Layer untouched. This will save both time and money. **It is always very important to properly isolate layers.**

> It is very important to isolate the layers in your project.

Although, theoretically, this all sounds very interesting and makes sense, it takes time and experience to fully understand how to isolate layers and, sometimes, for some functions, it can be quite difficult to decide to which layer they belong. You will have to use your best judgment to ensure that each feature lands on the proper layer. It is not enough to know that interaction features go on the presentation layer, functional features go on the business layer, and dependency or platform features are left for the backend API and platform layers. The problem is that, sometimes, a few features can appear to be somewhere in the middle. It is not infrequent that slight changes in architecture have to be made to accommodate for such changes. It is not a case of wrong planning and poor software design or engineering. **In every project you will face unexpected problems, very frequently out of your control, which will force you to rethink details of the architecture.**

> Be prepared for the need of rethinking parts of the architecture.

Whoever says that good planning never faces unexpected setbacks, is either someone with much to learn who never did anything serious, was just very lucky or an incompetent who has no idea what kind of a time bomb he left lurking in the code. Even if it is because of human error, it is in the human nature that we will miss things and that no amount of planning can account for every single problem one may face. That's why there are rules, processes and techniques. Not only to help with the development process but, also, to help the team detect any problems and trace back their origins, as well as to allow it to correct them. What you should do is to prepare your code to gracefully deal with the unpredictable problems in a wild-card fashion (and most likely gracefully fail) and to log every bit of information as possible. And even then, there will always be the possibility of events completely out of your control, even if it comes down to a meteor hitting the computer. Even the highest grade military quality software will have bugs or other problems, some of them could not be accounted for at the time of planning, sometimes not even during development, for a number of reasons and not all of them are the responsibility of the development team. Software development, as a science, is relatively new. It is one of the most rapidly changing and evolving sciences. The same happens with hardware, which, in some areas, evolves faster than the software developed for it can keep up with, and that leaves the developers in tight spots. On the other hand, in other areas, it is software that evolves faster and demands more computing power faster than hardware can keep up with.

2.2 Project management tools

It is very important for any developer to be perfectly aware of the tools at his disposal and to learn how to get the most of them. There are several software tools designed to help the developer build his projects and increase his productivity to the most. There are several categories of tools which need to be explored. They can help you with many peripheral tasks so that you can focus as much as possible in writing good code and avoid wasting time.

2.2.1 Code Editors and IDEs

As a developer, you will be writing code. For that, you'll need some kind of text editor. There are many available at your disposal, from the simplest ones to the most fully featured ones. **Be aware that the best editor is the one that works for you.** However, if you still want some advice and, especially, if you are new to programming, It's advisable to stay away from some of the most fully featured IDEs[2] for a simple reason: they may be confusing by offering too many options and functionalities. It is, without a doubt, bad not to have enough functionality but, sometimes, it can be worse to have too much. Too much options to which you are not used to may be counter-productive since that situation has the potential to cause you to feel lost while trying to find the functions you need to use. There are many development environments with just the right features needed to get started. Some of them are simple text editors on steroids, some others are trimmed down versions of fully featured professional environments. So, if you need this book, you most likely would be better off starting with one of the most simpler ones.

> The best code editor is the one that works for you.

Before exploring some examples, you should be aware of some of the basic features you may find to be useful in a development environment:

---

2 *Integrated Development Environment*

- Syntax highlighting and brace matching: these features help you track syntax errors and missing brackets or quotation marks. Even if you are an experienced programmer, these features will still be helpful. It is not just a question of pretty colors. Syntax highlighting is a very simple and relatively efficient way to help you realize your mistakes while you are coding.
- Code completion: writing code can become a tedious task, especially when you are required to write some things very often like variable or type names. Code completion helps you by providing in-line predictions of what you might want to write and the choice to accept the suggestion or keep writing. This saves time and effort by reducing the amount of typing needed.
- Code indenting and formating: code needs to be easy to understand and much of the readability depends on the formatting of the code. An editor with automatic code indenting and formatting abilities will help you keep your code clean and readable.
- Internationalization: with today's globalization and the existence of the Internet, it is much easier to expand businesses to foreign markets. This implies that you need to be prepared to supply such markets and their local cultures and languages. Besides, you should not be limited to a unique set of localized settings, because you have your own culture and language.
- Regular expression search: if you have such an option at your disposal, you'll have an easier life when the time comes (and believe me, it will come) to search not for a specific string but for an expression that could match a

variable, but predictable, pattern.
- Find in Files: This will allow you to search the whole project for a specific pattern. It is especially useful for finding places where certain symbols are used or "**TODO**" items yet to resolve.

If you're developing under Windows, maybe you should start with Dev-C++. Microsoft's Visual C++ Express may also be a good start, but remember that, as an IDE, it already features much of the functions from the full Visual Studio Suite. If you're developing under any flavor of a Unix-based system, like Linux or BSD, a good starting point could be Geany or Kate. Geany is a very simple IDE developed over GTK[3] and, a rather complete and intuitive environment for most users. KATE, on the other hand, is one of those IDEs that are more similar to a text editor on steroids. It is very easy to use and provides all the basic functionalities a developer should expect, as well as some more advanced ones. However, if you're more comfortable with the advanced features and you're craving for something more complete, while programming under Unix based environments, a suggestion would be KDevelop. Functionality-wise, it gets pretty close to Microsoft Visual Studio. None of the suggested IDEs will be explored in detail, because it is beyond the scope of this book.

Many seasoned developers will try to evangelize you on the virtues of Vi (or most likely Vim) and Emacs. The question is: why should we go back in time when you have at your disposal new tools with new features, that better integrate with your work environment and are less complicated to use? Vim and

---

[3] *The GIMP ToolKit is a set of libraries and components for user interface development.*

Emacs may have evolved, but you need to have the computer working for you, not the other way around. You need to boost your productivity to the maximum and that will surely be hard to achieve should you need to get used to a few dozen different environments, instead of being used to one with standardized features and interaction methods. But, in the end, as said before, you choose what you think feels right. And, unless it is a job requirement, don't let anybody else choose for you.

2.2.2 Version management

An adequate development process implies the existence of a revision control system. It is imperative to use such a system to assure the quality of the product. This doesn't apply only to large teams, but also to individual developers. A revision control system, or version management system, allows you to keep track of changes, the persons who made them, rollback any unwanted editions, and to setup checkpoints on features that are deemed stable. A VCS is also one of the tools a large distributed team needs to function properly, by allowing team members to remotely submit and inspect revisions of the project's contents. There are several different VCS suites. Some notable ones are the following:

> It is imperative to use a version control system.

- CVS: seems to be losing momentum. It was built on the original RCS revision control system.
- Subversion: SVN, for short, was developed to overcome many of the flaws and shortcomings of CVS. It has a lot more features than CVS and has been widely spread.

- GIT: It was originally developed in 2005 by Linus Torvalds to replace the commercial BitKeeper system the Linux Kernel team used to have in place. It is a distributed version control system. Thanks to being developed by Torvalds and being used for the development process of the Linux Kernel, it quickly gained popularity.

Features vary from one VCS to another, but the ones you're most likely going to need can be expected from any decent system. Those are:
- Project awareness: a lot of older VCS suites were not really project-aware. They worked in a more file oriented fashion. A project can be either a random collection of files or an organized collection of targets. Targets are the final products of processing the source files of the project. Most projects have a single target which can be a library, an executable, a document or some other production, but it is not uncommon to find projects with multiple targets. Also, it is logical that you should be able to isolate sub-projects within projects. Files and folders belonging to a project are assigned a log, which registers the history of changes made to those objects. It is common to have also logs for the entire project. For some systems, each project is called a repository. For others, the repository is the collection of projects it manages.
- Importing: projects consist of an (usually[4]) organized collection of files and those must come from somewhere. Although there are a few systems that

---

4 *Unfortunately... not always.*

allow you to create the files directly on the project's repository either as an empty stub or with preset basic contents based on skeleton file[5], not all let you do this. But all systems allow you to import a file to the project. Importing adds a file to the repository and subjects it to revision control.

- Removing: interestingly, although this might feel like a basic feature that every VCS should have, there were those which lacked the ability to actually remove files from the repository. Some others lack the ability to rename them or to manage folders properly. It sounds strange, but, well, it happens that some files lose usefulness within a project and need to be disposed of. And apparently, not every VCS developer thought this might be important.

- Check out or update: this feature has the same name in pretty much every VCS that currently exists. But it makes sense. The "check out" function allows you to obtain the latest or even a particular revision of the project or of a particular file or set of files from that project. You need to be aware that some systems use a locking scheme. This means that if, for example, you check out a particular file in the project, that file will be locked and nobody else will be able edit it. In the case of such systems, this sometimes avoids the need to deal with merge operations (described further in). You will need to check the file in (see below) so that others can work on it. Locking has lost supporters in favor of

---

[5] *Skeleton files are usually files with no actual useful content other than a predetermined layout for what the file might contain*

merging because in large teams it becomes counter-productive.
- Check in or commit: new versions of the files in the project need to be submitted to the repository to have its log registered as well as become available to other developers and to yourself.
- Merging: this allows you to work without the need to use locks in files you check out. This way, more than one person can work on the same file but only the first to commit it is able to do it without further action. Anyone that commits their changes after someone else did, will be required to merge the changes. If the version control system asks you to merge your changes and you refuse to do so, your version of the file will overwrite the version that was submitted before for the same revision.
- Branching: branching is a very interesting feature of a VCS. It allows you to fork (branch) the project's source so you can safely work on correcting bugs or implementing other features without interfering with the main source tree and vice-versa.
- Tagging or labeling: version control systems usually choose either a random name for the revisions of the files or a sequential number. However, you can tag or label a specific revision to make it easier to recall. You can, for instance, call it "Version1.0" or "ReleaseCandidate3", or whatever you find appropriate.

2.2.3 Project construction

To actually make your project usable, it needs to be built.

Building your project includes all the processes you perform to it after writing the source code: compiling, linking, and many other post processing steps. And building the project can be a very complex and tedious task. It would be nearly impossible to do so, if it weren't for some tools specialized in helping you manage the building stage. As the project grows in number of source files, it also grows in complexity and maintenance difficulty. It is, therefore, important to automate the task of transforming your art into a functioning product.

> You need helper tools to aid in the building stage.

Tools such as "**make**" allow you to write a description in the form of a mathematical model of the project's build process, so it can be automatically carried out whenever you need to build it. Dealing with "**make**" is actually quite the adventure. This tool has a temper and when it gets mad, it is rarely easy to understand why, since its messages are a bit cryptic. Basically, "**make**" behaves like a woman in PMS. In general, makefiles are based on a list of rules, one for each target. Those rules describe the target, the dependencies and the commands:

```
target: dependencies
        commands
```

The element "**target**" is usually the name of the file to be produced by the specific rule, although, however, that is not always the case. Sometimes, the target can actually be a virtual target, with the sole purpose of aggregating several targets to be produced in one run. The thing is, that despite the fact that "**make**" allows you to specify several targets in a single

"`Makefile`", unless you specify, in the command line, which targets are to be built, only the first target will be processed. It is common practice to add a target virtual target called "`all`" to the top of the "`Makefile`" and, in the dependencies, add all the targets that are to be built. The name of this target isn't really relevant as long as it is the first one. Since there will never be any file with that name, that target's dependencies will always be checked, since "`make`" deals with dependencies recursively.

It is not the purpose of this manual to provide you with a detailed explanation of how "`make`" works and how to write makefiles. I advise you to consult an appropriate reference, for that matter. But I will provide you some advice about using it. First, if you have a correctly written project file, you can put to good use all those cores your CPU has. This is because "`make`" allows you to specify how many concurrent processes you want it to run in parallel, by using a specialized command-line option. Second, with appropriate tweaking to your "`Makefile`" and some shell command tricks, instead of displaying the complete commands for each compiled file while the process is ongoing, you can have it printing only a summary of the information and being detailed only when errors occur. There's no need to fill up the screen with information which is unnecessary most of the times with the potential to cause confusion. Instead, you can have a more organized compilation process tracking printout. Third, apply to the file the same principles you apply to programming, by using variables and constants to reduce the amount of repeated code along the file. And fourth, learn about implicit rules, suffix rules, and the "`VPATH`" variable, as they allow you to simplify both your "`Makefile`" and your project directory, but be careful about naming collisions when dealing with that variable.

2.3 Project documentation

All projects require documentation. Some projects more than others, but all have it in one form or another, even if it comes down to just the comments on the code. This sub-chapter is about the stand-alone documentation.

2.3.1 Types of documentation

There are several types of documentation you need to be aware of. Although quite frequently they are overlooked or ignored, there are cases where you have no chance of escaping them because of the nature of your project, the company policy,

> Writing good documentation can be one of the most difficult tasks in a project.

or any number of legal reasons. If you're working for a company that works with critical systems or needs to have its products submitted to some kind of certification process, then that is one such situation. One thing that is required from all documents is a clear language that allows the reader to immediately understand what the writer meant. It is not always easy to achieve such feat, in part because the fact that this area is so technical, creates, just by itself, several difficulties.

2.3.1.1 Product specification

The **product specification is the most basic type of documentation projects require.** It describes, in detail, the features the product should have and the behaviors it should display. It is usually a list of topics about your product and results from working closely with the client, understanding his needs. Even if it is not a case of software made to order, your company does have clients. In the case of custom designed software, your client will describe to you what he needs and, together, you'll come up with a list of characteristics that describe the software. If you're building software to be available off the shelf to a large number of customers, the case of a specific market segment, then you build the specification based upon the studies the marketing department in your company will perform by analyzing the needs of a sample of the market segment. In any case, you may end up being part of the team that builds the specification and, if you're a programmer, you will always be part of the team that needs to develop the software based on that document. This document needs to be easy to understand both by the developers, the architects and the client. It is usually the only document about the internals of the product that all participants in a software development process have access to, including the client.

> A product specification is imperative.

2.3.1.2 High Level Architecture

The high level architecture document is an internal document which explains, from a very high level, the way the software product is supposed to work by means of describing without a great deal of detail, the functional blocks that it is made of. It should contain UML diagrams of the major components of the product and a textual description of them and the way they communicate. It should also identify the actors present in the interaction with the product.

2.3.1.3 Low Level Architecture

The low level architecture document provides a more detailed explanation about what the high level architecture document explained. It explains everything at a level that goes quite close to code. It can even identify some of the procedures that need to be written to address the requirements listed in the project specification. It is the document that more closely describes the application of the items in the product specification. It takes the project apart and describes everything to the smallest detail possible short of already describing code. Both this and the high level architecture document can be organized in a different fashion that explains, in some way, the different aspects of the project, regarding data, component interaction and procedural components.

2.3.1.4 Application Programming Interface

The application programming interface is more important to the developers of the project unless the product is supposed to provide ways other developers can use for their products to interact with yours. The Application Programming Interface is, as explained before in a footnote, a set of classes, function calls, macros, variables and values that a software product uses to interact with another software product. Software products, in this case, might be your product and something built by someone else with no relation to your

> Just because an API is usually internal, doesn't mean you can take shortcuts while documenting and organizing it.

team, or they might sub-products or elements of your product. Having a properly defined and documented API for your product is important, not only to users of your product, but also to you and your team. Apart from the comments in the code, this is usually the lowest level documentation there is about your product. There are some tools that will be explored in more detail in section 2.3.2, such as Doxygen, that extract documentation directly from the code. Although the value of that tool is undeniable, it is not recommended filling up the code with too much comments. Comments longer than one or two lines about anything start to insert bloat that actually complicates the code and makes it more difficult to be humanly interpreted. Although a lot of this might be just a question of politics, writing proper and extensive documentation of the code separately and providing only trivial guidance comments in the code itself is usually a better policy.

2.3.1.5 Product manual

The product manual is, as you may understand, one of the most problematic documents your project will have. The reason is simple. The product is made by developers, who have technical knowledge. The manual is intended for the end user which, depending on the type of product, usually has no type of technical knowledge at all. This poses a dilemma. Who is supposed to write the product manual? Because of the wrong choices when answering this question, a lot of products come with sub-satisfactory manuals and the situation gets further complicated when translations are written. The first trait to look for when choosing someone to write the product manual is a good domain of the primary language on which the manual is to be written. Then, that person must have some technical knowledge but needs not be the foremost expert. Just enough to be able to understand the language used by the developers. It is a good policy to team a competent writer with the team manager or someone with a good general knowledge about the project, someone that knows with precision how the product specification was actually implemented. And, in the end, the manual should be tried and reviewed by someone external to the project, usually a team, so that a non-tainted mind, someone impartial, unbiased and with no knowledge of the product can actually try it under circumstances that are as close as possible to the end user.

> Writing product manuals is difficult because developers know too much about the project to realize what the user will fail to understand.

2.3.1.6 Online help

The online help, where applicable, suffers from the same problem as the user manual since it actually is a form of user manual. The online help can take many forms: an HTML page, tooltips that popup when the mouse passes over a certain control, a text screen you get when you select the help choice in a CLI program and many more. The type of help system in your project must be carefully chosen. Since no one can be good at everything, good programmers usually aren't that good at designing user interfaces, especially not graphical ones. It is important that your team has someone properly qualified to deal with user experience. And that someone is more than likely someone who can properly design the online help system.

2.3.1.7 Safety warnings

Every product requires some sort of safety warning. Products sold in the European Union, for example, must conform to CE guidelines. While software, in itself, may seem harmless, because it can't really do anything unless installed, when deployed in a working machine, software can do any number of things. Remember that besides your home computer, software also powers vehicles, medical equipment, satellites, space stations and, also, very powerful weapons. Safety warnings should be applied in accordance to the specific industry and usage. For example, a simple game, which apparently might pose no threat, can, in fact, be a risk to children, if it contains improper language or mature content. It is not a life threatening situation, but it is a risk to the education and proper development of the children exposed to it. Also, in a more exquisite situation, some light and sound patterns may influence and trigger seizures in people suffering from epilepsy, which, despite being a long shot, it is not unheard of, not only in games, but also in television cartoons.

> Some software products demand specific safety labels, forcing you to refer to local legislation.

But this is not all. Some types of software, and even algorithms, are considered, by some governments, as ammunition, despite being apparently harmless. One blatant example of this situation is the case of encryption software and algorithms. For a long time, PGP, a symmetric key based encryption software, was under a prohibition to be exported and some algorithms still are.

2.3.2 Helper tools

Generating documentation is a complicated, tedious and long process, but also important in your project. It is already hard enough to come up with the stuff that has to be written, but it is would be much worse if you don't have tools to aid you in producing such information. Therefore here are some you might find useful.

2.3.2.1 Doxygen

While it's not advisable to have the code overrun by long detailed comments to be caught by these tools, Doxygen, and similar programs, have their merits. Besides, Doxygen doesn't only extract information from your comments. It is also able to produce a reflection of the API you created and schematics of the class hierarchies in your project. Doxygen allows you to produce documentation for a wide range of languages (including C, C++. C#, PHP, Java, Objective-C, Python and even some hardware description languages), in a few different formats (HTML, LaTex offline references, RTF, PostScript and even compressed HTML – MS CHM – and Unix manual pages). This system is very flexible and makes it easy to visualize relations between elements in the source, which enables you to easily navigate the source of large projects. Additionally, it allows you to put your documentation somewhere else, should you want Doxygen to produce your full API documentation, but still avoid overloading the code with text.

2.3.2.2 Wikis

Using a "Wiki" is always an interesting option. It allows you to document everything in your project. Your team can have a place to store all the information, all the manuals and this facilitates the collective effort of writing them. There are several available systems, both free and commercial and, although they somewhat differ in the syntax and the way they are implemented, the basic principle behind them is always the same: a system that enables you, and your team, to write online documents using some kind of markup language.

2.3.2.3 Visio, Dia

Visio (for Windows) and Dia (mostly for everything else) are software packages for producing the diagrams needed to either document or design the software product. Visio is a commercial Microsoft product, Dia is an open source package. In order to be done right, your project will need many diagrams in the documentation. You'll need them to document the API, to document the interaction between the elements in the product and to document the functional blocks in the architecture files.

2.4 Deploying your project

After your product is finalized, it is time to introduce it to the market. You need to make it available and the method you choose will depend on the target client and on the requirements of your product. You'll have to consider the distribution policy, licensing, methods, documentation and support. And, today, the need to provide support and the new means available to us have brought severe changes in deployment policies and methodologies. While, not long ago, you would have to pay for updates and would receive them as hard copies, today your computer automatically performs updates, sometimes without you even knowing it. Of course, this can't be applied to all systems because each case has its own intricacies, but for general home/office computing, you will, undoubtedly, have already been exposed to examples of such systems. Microsoft, Mozilla and Adobe are all examples of product brands that employ such a method.

2.4.1 Deployment policy and licensing

How much are you going to charge for your product? Everything has a price, and why? Because software costs to develop. Developing a software product takes resources such as equipment, energy, personnel. Even if you're doing it as an hobby, you are spending money to do so. If you are deploying it, make sure you take something back, even if it is the joy of having a satisfied user base.

Are you going to release the source code or only binaries? It is important that you understand the advantages and disadvantages of each way.

Who will be allowed to access your product? Who is the end user? Before you deploy a product, before you even think of developing it, you need to have a market segment for it. You may be your own market segment or you may intend to satisfy a specific need of a specific group of people. And, of course, you need to determine, from those possible users, who are the ones that will be eligible. It may be a question of filling a specified prerequisite, even if such prerequisite is just the price they will pay.

Are you selling them the product or a user license? If you are developing to satisfy a market segment, then you are keeping the ownership of the product and you are offering that market segment only the possibility of acquiring a license to use the product. However, if you are producing for a specific customer, you may not have the choice of deciding whether you are handing out a license or the ownership of the product. In this case, you may have to relinquish the rights to all the data produced. Of course, everything is negotiable and this situation is no different.

2.4.2 Deployment methods

Deciding which deployment method to use is also part of the entire process. You are building a product for somebody, therefore you must devise a way to make your product reach that entity.

2.4.2.1 Binary versus source

Most commercial products in the market nowadays are delivered this way, regardless of being distributed over the wire or as physical media. Binary packages allow for some degree of intellectual property protection by not explicitly exposing the source code of a software product. They also have the advantage of reducing dependencies on additional tools to make them usable on the target machines as they come ready to use. On the other hand, they can't be optimized *in loco* for each of the target machines, as they must be generic enough for all of the machines present in the target market segment.

Distribution as a source package, on the other hand, allows you to have the product compiled in the client's machines. This way the client can either have it compiled in the target machine directly, or compile it in another computer and perform the deployment afterwards. Your customer will be able to select specific optimizations suitable to his needs and your product will be adapted to the final host machine instead of you having to deploy a binary that may have to be shipped without hardware specific optimizations. However, this implies that your customer will be able to skim through your sources, even if you attempt to use some sort of mechanism to prevent him to do so. There is always a way to go around this. And this also implies that you have to make sure that your client has, on his platform, all the elements necessary to compile the product. This includes compilers, libraries, headers and any other relevant media.

2.4.2.2 Hard copies versus network

Distributing a software product in physical media is something that used to have more fans. However, the difficulties associated with using physical media, as well as the cost, have been increasingly justifying shifting towards networked distribution methods. For a lot of software products. it is, nowadays, possible to acquire their licenses over the Internet, and to download the product for installation when necessary. The license usually gets associated to a person, a company, or a machine and usage restrictions are all defined in the licensing policy.

Hard copies can contain whatever you like, be it source or binaries. You'll have to decide how to include the product documentation, and whether you'll ship a printed manual or digital documents in a CD or DVD. You'll have to design a box and a label, include bar codes and produce the media. Of course, you can always outsource all of this, nevertheless it implies additional costs to production. You'll also have to consider about delivery and the fact that it may be hard to get to some of your potential clients this way, as delivery routes for physical media aren't always reliable or efficient.

Having it on the network cuts costs on physical production and distribution but implies building an infrastructure capable of handling all the requests, and exacerbates the need for well maintained security systems to protect your intellectual property.

2.5 The team

The success of a product depends entirely on its team. The team is more than a bunch of developers stuck in a room. The team is composed of the developers, designers, marketing and advertisement experts, lawyers and leaders. If done right, you could sell snake oil for gold. If done wrong, you will be unable to have your market segment accept diamonds even if your handing them out for free.

> The success of a product depends entirely on its team.

2.5.1 Interaction

Depending on the project, there are several ways to organize your team and steer the interaction of its members. Many companies are now opting for open spaces instead of individual offices for their employees. This facilitates communication and interaction. It doesn't come without flaws, of course, one of them being the fact that, in an open space, privacy and a quiet environment are a bit difficult to achieve. The kind of space you'll be in will greatly depend on the project but, a lot of times, it will depend on company policy and may not always be the best choice for that particular project or even for that company. **It is important that you learn to adapt to each situation, if you don't already have that skill. The life cycle of a project implies that restructuring is inevitable.**

Adaptability can be your most valuable skill.

More importantly, it is imperative that you respect your team mates and your team leader (or your subordinates, should you be the team leader). Even if you don't agree with your boss, you need to remember that there are proper ways to address such disagreements. If you're in a brainstorming session, then it will probably be inoffensive to disagree with your team leader if you're just exchanging ideas. However, from the moment your boss gives you a direct order with which you don't agree, unless you want to actively sabotage your team, you have two choices. You are either polite and ask your boss about it in the most discrete manner possible, or you wait until you are able to address him privately. If done any other way, you'll be undermining the authority of your leader and the team's cohesion. If that happens, the team will start to fall apart and don't expect that to turn out to be good for you, since most of the times you will be fingered as being the saboteur, and you will probably be let go.

2.5.2 Communication

There are several means you can use to share information

inside the team. **Communication is not just talking with one another, it is also making documentation available so members of the team can access it.**
For real time communication, you can either address the person/persons directly, especially if they work in the same office or building, or you can use a typical real time communication system like written chat, phone or VoIP. When using such systems, it is important to have them set up in such a way as to make team communication as easy as possible. Usually, internal communication systems allow the company to set up networks and groupings for this. Another way to communicate with your team, despite not actually looking like that, is a network share. While it may seem rudimentary, in a time when we have so many mechanisms for sharing information, it is actually not. Inside a corporate network, a networked folder is actually a pretty effective way to share some types of documents or files not appropriate to send by mail or some other way because of any of its characteristics.

> Team communication depends on several different tools.

When sending e-mails, remember to be concise and direct. Remember that it is easy to mislead a person even unwillingly. Letting this situation happen because we didn't care is just plain stupid and will cause problems to the team, delays, maybe even have nefarious consequences in the quality of the final product. Keep copies of all the e-mails you send as, sooner or later, you may end up needing them. And, while trust is an important feeling to develop in a team, never expect anyone to behave by what was only word of mouth. Important decisions, questions, reminders and other data should always be appropriately registered, even if only in a simple e-mail. If anything important was discussed verbally, immediately after that discussion, send an e-mail to that person with your interpretation of that conversation and ask the person to acknowledge it.

For sure, the team will have internal documents and memos that need to be available for everyone or even may be a collective effort to write. For such situations, using a content management system or, better yet, a Wiki, is a good policy. Not only it allows sharing the documents to the whole team, but it is also easy to use, without being very time consuming. Wikis are easily available and, if required, most of them allow you to set up special permissions, depending on the access levels of each team member or add new features.

> Centralizing user management is a major advantage for team coordination.

One very important aspect of team communication, is centralizing user and information management. The reason for this is that it makes it much easier to organize everything, diluting the need to individually manage each subsystem of the infrastructure that supports the team, greatly reducing management tasks to a bare minimum and ensuring synchronization between all the systems. This also increases accountability, improves security and facilitates the legitimate access to information. Most, if not all, today's network oriented data management systems support directory services, if not directly, at least through their specific plug-in systems. Directory services are centralized databases about the resources of an institution, with the important characteristic that they are intended primarily to be consulted. They are excellent choices as centralized authentication and authorization management systems. Examples of such systems are LDAP[6] and Microsoft Active Directory[7]. Having in place centralization and synchronization policies is a strong and important step towards achieving adequate team interaction.

2.5.3 Hiring

If you're leading a team, it is likely you'll have to hire new people or recruit them from other sections of the institution you're in. There are certain qualities you'll need in each of your subordinates and some others that are applicable only to certain positions in your team. So, it is important to know the right questions to ask and how to interpret both the answers and the reactions of your candidates. For the untrained eye, these are difficult to spot during an interview but, with the right questions, all the relevant traits may show up if you pay attention. Intuition and experience, in due time, will show results. However, don't expect to become an expert. A very important skill in anyone, even in a boss, is to know when and how to ask for help. So, it may be a good thing if you ask for help from one of the other team members. Not only they may have a bit more intuition when dealing with people, but they may also notice some traits you didn't, for a number of reasons, or devise relevant context-based questions.

You should have your interviews properly organized, structured and planned. This is, in no way, an impediment to a little subtle deviation from the order of your questions, should you find it relevant. Between sixty and ninety minutes

---

6 *Lightweight Directory Access Protocol*
7 *In layman's terms, it can be considered a superset of LDAP, but it actually includes modified or improved versions of standard protocols.*

is usually the ideal time to interview a good candidate. A bad one will often have been excluded after half an hour.

> Don't stick to a simple classic "who are you and what have you done" interview. Make the applicant experience the conditions to be expected on the workplace, while testing his knowledge, intelligence and emotions.

Start the interview with some non-technical questions about the life and past experience of the applicant, and then go on to some character evaluation questions. Evaluate his creativity, making him complete sentences, for example. Try some emotional intelligence exercises and, only then, fire away the technical questions. The order for this method was not a random choice. The objective is to gradually get the candidates more tired as they approach the end of the interview, so you can see how they react while trying to solve technical problems and riddles after having undergone through a mental ordeal and being subjected to several different, sometimes randomly chosen, pressure factors. These interviewing techniques work quite well, with results that are more than satisfactory.

2.5.3.1 Pressure factors

One thing important during interviews is to add environmental pressure factors to test your applicants abilities to cope with the pressure they may naturally find in the workplace. On many companies this is especially important, because the programmers have to be able to produce excellent code under extraordinary pressure circumstances like, for instance, deadlines. Having the candidate solve the problems in a white board will give him the sense of pressure of the school years, when he would be called to solve problems in front of the class. Threatening to fail him immediately should he allow the pen to dry while he is thinking how to solve the problem, is one way to introduce some humor, but at the same time, introduces one more pressure factor and a way to evaluate his ability to be disciplined by checking whether he puts the cap back on to respect what you just said. Always let him know that you wouldn't submit him to a problem you hadn't already solved yourself and, if you threatened him before, remember to give him a treat and allow him an apparently easy way to win by telling him that if he manages to solve one of the emotional intelligence problems faster than you did when you attempted to solve them, that he had the job.

> Have your interviews prepared, but introduce slight deviations to catch the applicant off-guard.

Try sounds. Think of songs and noise that could be found in the workplace. Having the theme song from "Jeopardy" playing while waiting for their answers or while they were attempting to solve a problem. Have food in the room and let him watch you have a meal, while he is trying to solve the problems. Why? Because in a lot of workplaces, with an open space environment, they should be expected to gracefully handle pressure situations and to be able to not be distracted from what the co-worker on the next desk is doing. Sometimes, the co-workers may need to stay in pulling extra hours and having meals in the office to save time. And the food odors, the noise from the other desks and every other aspect of these events should not prevent them from being at their best.

Besides what has already been said, having a team mate to

help you with the interviews is important for more reasons than those already mentioned. If done right, it introduces that nice additional factor called "good cop, bad cop". Psychological games are always an effective way to both test and manipulate people. Using the "good cop, bad cop" technique, you'll not only get to understand how much pressure they require and how much they can take, but also what motivates your applicants – if they are more susceptible to the comfort of the positive reinforcement or to the fear of being punished. How? Done right, the "bad cop" would ask the question. Both interviewers would be constantly paying attention to check his reactions. If the fear of the "bad cop" doesn't make the candidate get things right, maybe the protecting sensation of the "good cop" offering the candidate a "comfort zone" will get the answer out of him. Be sure to keep alternating, with each question, the "cop" you use.

2.5.3.2 Learn to read them

Ask them what they feel are their most important virtues and flaws and briefly analyze each of them. Have them explain each item. Be ready to predict answers from your applicant, well enough to have new questions prepared based on his response. Context questions are a good idea because many of them can catch the applicant off-guard, being especially useful to detect trained answers. Because of trained answers, it is important to subject all the applicants to mind games and riddles, to test their emotional intelligence. If they are using trained answers, then they are lying to you. What you want most in your team is a person that can be honest and straightforward. Pre-planned answers leave the applicant with little room to expand his horizons during the interview, and that usually translates to a person with little imagination and a reduced ability to deal with situations in real time.

There are some traits you'll need to look for in your applicants. Flexibility, adaptability and ability to learn are amongst the most important ones. While nobody can be good at everything, and it is usually the best policy to specialize in some specific subject, it is also important that all of the team members have at least a small bit of understanding about other areas and the ability to easily switch and adapt to different tasks. This not only improves communication inside the team, reducing misunderstandings, but also, if the team gets reduced or more effort is needed in some particular aspect of the project, it becomes easier to reinforce the workforce allocated to it. Generally, more than already acquired knowledge, you'll want someone with a flexible mind, with a very high ability to learn and understand new things. This way you can induce your subordinates into focusing their learning abilities on the most important subjects to the project. Although people with a very high level of knowledge are mostly always a good asset, knowledge is something gained with time. But, during that time, a person develops habits, some of which may be undesirable in your team. One thing all teams need is consistency. And some seasoned programmers usually have already developed some habits and programming practices of their own that may clash with your team's guidelines.

People come in every sizes, colors and shapes. **However, the only kind of people you don't want in your team, is the kind that doesn't know what chain of command and team**

> Don't hesitate in excluding "underminers" from your team.

spirit means. Those persons undermine all the efforts to keep the team together and, usually, do that by trying to steal away the respect the team has for you as their leader. Be smart in spotting those rotten apples and don't hesitate in excluding them from your team, if possible, before they even make part of it but, if not, at the first sign of trouble. Don't let anyone pull the rug from under your feet. **While being a leader gives you a position of power, it also makes you an easy and preferred target for some people with a weaker character.** If you're a leader, even the style, the way you dress, move and interact is important. When you're the boss, make sure you stand out and that you have presence. You need to be noted discretely and passively. Do not attempt to stand out artificially by imposing your presence. Have an attitude worthy of respect so that your underlings look up to you and aspire to be as good as you, both as a person and as a professional. Make sure you follow your team's progress and that you attend to their needs and reasonable requests for resources and training requirements.

> Being a leader makes you a target.

People with a personal agenda are not the only ones you should be careful about. You will also find people that, while not on purpose, just doesn't get along with other people and doesn't share the same notions of respect that you, and the other elements, uphold. They just have no idea of how inappropriate their behavior is. They can cause as much damage as someone who is actively trying to undermine you and sabotage the team. One example would be someone with the nerve to actually say to your face that he'd rather spend three hours trying to get someone to solve a problem, than spending those three hours solving it himself. That would be nice if needed someone for a managing position. Or someone arrogant enough to say that the problem of his interview going so bad was not that he wasn't good enough, but that you chose the wrong questions for the knowledge he had. Well, you might have chosen the wrong questions for his knowledge, but for sure you chose the right ones for the company's requirements. Don't be arrogant to the point of thinking the world has to adapt to you and not the other way around.

2.5.3.3 *Evaluate the dynamic response*

Don't expect your applicants to be right in every question. Let's be honest, even if you give them the entire ninety minutes to answer the questions, most of the problems used have the sole objective of understanding their minds. Although they may have the obligation to know some of the results by heart and to be right in some of the questions, try to present them with questions to test their deductive, math and reasoning skills, more than his knowledge. **It is more important to understand how he thinks than how much he memorized.** It is more important to have as a team member an intelligent person that knows how and when to consult technical references and documentation if necessary, than a person with weak reasoning skills even if he has memorized the entire Knuth's "Art of Computer Programming".

> It's more important to have a fast learner team member, than a slow one that memorized everything.

About the problems themselves, lateral thinking problems and puzzles are a good way to test both the deductive abilities and creativity. Most problems have several possible answers and they are all a good way to understand how a mind works and how it reacts. There are several books with problems of that kind that you could use to spice up your recruiting process.

Ask them questions that do not really have a single correct answer, only to understand how they justify their choice. One personal favorite is to ask them what would they most likely sacrifice, code quality in favor of respecting deadlines, or deadlines in favor of maintaining code quality. Although it would be preferred to keep code quality, it is no surprise that in corporate environments, top management demands quick results without having the slightest idea of how the development process evolves and that, a lot of times, forces good programmers into taking dangerous shortcuts.

> Use problems that target lateral thinking to test deductive abilities and creativity.

Then have him answer direct answers and apply that knowledge to problems that demand both that knowledge and deductive skills. There are several problems you can either devise or find that can help you with this. When hiring C++ programmers, it is recommended that you go for a bottom up approach, starting with the basics and ending with a more complex problem. This stage of the interviews could start with a question about boolean logic, and end up with a question that includes as much as knowledge as possible from the subjects they might face. A question that includes boolean logic, bitwise arithmetic, math, algorithms, code and a bit of computer architecture understanding is a good idea. Make it hard to solve, if possible so hard that they cannot answer it without some help. The most important thing about this question is that it will provide you with a strong insight on how your applicant would use the knowledge he had and the one you'd let him acquire during the resolution. Make it your policy to help people that actually make an effort and make life harder for the ones who just don't seem to try hard enough.

3 Code organization

Now this is going to hurt. As stated before, writing good software is not just about writing the code respecting syntax and semantics. Even if the written code has the best possible performance, it may still not be the best code. Good code is not just about performance. And it is never about presenting obfuscated solutions that merely look elegant. **Good code is also organized and readable, as well as properly documented and created following well thought**

> Good code is not just code that works.

guidelines and procedures. In time, your programming skills and methodologies will evolve. You will be learning a lot from your own mistakes (and hopefully, a lot more from everyone else's mistakes before you make them too).

3.1 Code formatting style

The code formatting style that is going to be presented is a tested style, already deployed in some professional environments and that has been used with much success. Where used, it allowed a quicker and easier integration of new team members to projects.

In any project, a concise and standardized set of guidelines is important to maintain things organized and the team members able to understand each other's work. You may devise a style more suitable to yourself, or possibly already have one. When working in a big project, unless you're the one making the rules, you may already be subject to a set of guidelines previously set in place by the managers of such project. In any case, the next suggestions are interesting ideas about good practices when organizing your code.

> Concise and standardized guidelines are important for the project to succeed.

3.1.1 Alignment

One of the most extensively discussed aspects of formatting code is the alignment. Alignment styles are like sexual organs. Every person has them and may be playing with their own or someone else's, whether they want it or not. This is a style which is actually quite common and that seems to work best for mostly everyone. It provides a very obvious way to track blocks and statement co-dependencies. Take a look at the following example:

```
switch(p_color)
{
  case(E_Colors_Red):
  {
    std::cout << "Red" << std::endl;
    break;
  }
  case(E_Colors_Green):
  {
    std::cout << "Green" << std::endl;
    break;
  }
  case(E_Colors_Blue):
  {
    std::cout << "Blue" << std::endl;
    break;
  }
  default:
  {
    std::cout
       << "A black hole ate your color"
       << std::endl;
  }
};
```

If you pay attention to this example, you'll notice that the opening brackets are always on the line that follows the statement they are linked to, and that the closing brackets are aligned with the opening brackets. This way, just by scrolling the cursor, or your eyes, down the same column, you always know where the block begins and where it ends, in an easy manner. It helps you keep the code maintainable and understandable, because it increases readability. And the brackets are also aligned with their master statements, which also helps you find where they come from. Many people put the opening bracket at the end of its statement line, however, that may actually decrease readability because it forces you to scan in both directions and, sometimes, in more than one line. You want productivity and that does not seem a good way to achieve it. Also, you will notice the usage of two spaces for indentation instead of four or a tabulation. Two spaces should be comfortable enough without spreading your code horizontally too much.

3.1.2 Spaces

Avoid using spaces either before or after parenthesis since they bring no readability benefit. You'll just be wasting space(s) with them. Since coding is most frequently done using a mono-spaced font and parenthesis are a thin character, the empty area they leave unused in their character space is usually enough.

```
1  int add(int p_lhs, int p_rhs)
2  {
3    return(p_lhs + p_rhs);
4  }
```

On comma-separated lists, a space after a comma, but never before, is a good choice. Although that may be more of an aesthetic choice than a practical one, but does not influence practicality and looks quite nice, also allowing comforting readability. It is the typically used scheme when using commas to write texts in natural language, which may, anyway, come more naturally. However, make sure every operator is isolated from each of its operands with one space. It is important to give some prominence to operators so they are easier to spot and follow.

3.1.3 Brackets

You may have noticed, in the example from section 3.1.1, that there are parenthesis isolating the case statement's predicates (the values they test for). This is done with the "`return`" and "`throw`" statements as well, by writing them like this:

```
return(true);
```

The reason for this is simple. It's one more trick of discipline you should aspire to dominate. Exceptions are a bad thing. Not the concept of C++ Exceptions, but exceptions to rules. A statement that takes a parameter and does not enforce the usage of parenthesis to enclose the parameter is an exception to the syntax, since most other statements do (like "`if`", "`while`", "`catch`") and all functions definitely do. This means that, sometimes, you will, end up writing something that actually requires brackets without them, making you lose time recompiling when the compiler reaches that error. Besides, it also helps with readability, so that you can quickly and easily spot what is actually being passed to that statement, should you, for some reason, need to write a complex expression and more than one statement in one line. The "`case`" statement's code has also been isolated using curly bracket blocks. This has been done for similar reasons. Although it is not a requirement of the "`case`" statement, it improves readability and strengthens your discipline.

3.2 Header files logic

You should not mix declarations and code. You shouldn't even have them in the same file. Declarations should be left for a header file, the "`.h`" file, and the code for the "`.c`" or "`.cpp`" file. If you are working with C++, having dedicated sets of "`.h`" and "`.cpp`" files for each class is a very efficient way of achieving containment and to organize your code. This will, however, significantly increase the number of files in your project, but has the nice side effect of better isolating the code segments of the project and potentially reduce conflicts while submitting new revisions of the project to the repository, which implies that merging needs will also be reduced.

> Don't mix declarations and code.

It is appropriate that the files are named after the class they hold. Imagine that you have a class named "`CWindow`". You would, then, have a file named "`CWindow.h`", which would hold the class declaration, and the file "`CWindow.cpp`", with the class implementation. Having classes split like this also provides you with increased selectivity during compilation. This means that you can control which files you want to include and reduce compilation time (and probably the size of your code) by including only the class headers you use in each of your project's modules. It is a better way to go instead of having all the class declarations in a single file.

Problems you might encounter are header recursion and header repetition. An header "`a.h`" that includes another header "`b.h`" which, in turn, includes the header "`a.h`" again, for example. You need to avoid having the declarations made on the "`a.h`" header file repeated when "`b.h`" includes "`a.h`". You may face situations like this, most likely not as simple, but as a long chain of dependencies. You may also face repetition of header inclusions. Suppose, now, the situation of having the header files "`a.h`" and "`b.h`". Imagine also that you include both of them in your project and that they both include an header "`c.h`". The result is that, by recursion, your file will be including the file "`c.h`" twice. You don't need the declarations made in "`c.h`" twice. Your compiler won't even accept them and will present you with error messages for duplicate definitions. How do you avoid this situation, then?

> Beware of header recursion and header repetition

Well, to solve that problem, you resort to a very powerful weapon of your compiler: the preprocessor. The preprocessor allows you to define constructs for conditional compilation. So, you use macros and preprocessor conditionals. Take, for example, the following fictitious "`c.h`" header file:

```
1  #ifndef __C_H__
2  #define __C_H__
3  ...
4  // source of your file
5  ...
6  #endif
```

Assume that the lines 3 to 5 correspond to the actual source code you want on your header file. Everything you have from line 2 to line 5 included, will only be seen by the compiler if the macro "`__C_H__`" has not yet been defined. That's what the "`#ifndef <macro>`" directive means. If the macro is not defined, then the preprocessor will allow the compiler to see everything from that line to the corresponding "`#endif`". You can see that the "`__C_H__`" macro is only defined inside the "`#ifndef-#endif`" block, which implies that it will only be defined once, even if the file is included multiple times because, once it is defined, the "`#ifndef __C_H__`" will prevent the preprocessor from entering that block of code and will, therefore, ignore everything inside it. Some compilers also have specific extensions to the preprocessor that allow you to do this with a single directive. With the Microsoft compilers, you can, for example, just use the "`#pragma once`" directive which will do the same as the construct presented above. It basically tells the preprocessor to consider the file only once, despite how many times the file has been included. Regardless of that feature, defining a macro with the name of the file (the "`__C_H__`" in this example) is always a good idea.

3.3 File layout

The best way to create logical distinctions between areas within the files is to use the comments to do so. It makes sense that a file should be organized by sections that encapsulate logically similar elements. In a C or C++ file, there can be several sections. You may want to separate the preprocessor constructions (directives and macros), declarations (like custom types, classes, prototypes, constants and global variables), and the code (class methods and function implementations). More specifically, you should place everything but code in the ".h" file (a reasonable exception is inline code) and all the code in the ".cpp" file.

One simple advice is to use comments to draw dividing lines that help you distinguish between sections and to follow them religiously. Although it may look overkill and make small files look big and bloated, it actually makes them really organized and with the help of skeleton files, managing them becomes really easy. This is an example of an organized header file:

```
// source/folder/CObject.h - short description
// From package PackageName
// 2008+ The institution
// 2008+ First guy who worked on this file
// 2008+ Second guy who worked on this file

// ===================================================
// PT: pré-processador
// EN: pre-processor
// ===================================================

#ifndef __MYPROJECT_H__
#error "Can only be used from within MyProject.h"
#else
#ifndef __MYPROJECT_COBJECT_H__
#define __MYPROJECT_COBJECT_H__



// ===================================================
// PT: estruturas e tipos
// EN: structures and types
// ===================================================
```

```
25
26   // ---------------------------------------------------
27   // PT: cores diferentes
28   // EN: different colors
29
30   enum E_Colors
31   {
32     E_Colors_Min = 0,
33
34     E_Colors_Red,          // red
35     E_Colors_Green,        // green
36     E_Colors_Blue,         // blue
37
38     E_Colors_Unknown,
39
40     E_Colors_Max
41   };
42
43
44   // ---------------------------------------------------
45   // PT: estrutura de demonstração
46   // EN: case study structure
47
48   typedef struct
49   {
50     E_Colors m_color1;
51     E_Colors m_color2;
52
53     char * m_name;
54
55   } TMaterial;
56
57   // ===================================================
58   // PT: declaração da classe
59   // EN: class declaration
60   // ===================================================
61
62   class CObject
63   {
```

```
64      // constructor and visibility declarations
65      // deliberately missing
66
67      TMaterial * m_material;
68
69      float m_x, m_y, m_z, m_scale;
70
71      // PT: ampliar o objecto
72      // EN: zoom the object
73      bool zoom(float p_scale);
74
75      // PT: mover o objecto
76      // EN: move the object
77      bool move(float p_x, float p_y, float p_z);
78
79  };
80
81
82
83  #endif
84  #endif
85
86
87
88  // ====================================================
89  // === EOF ============================================
90  // ====================================================
91
```

Now, for an explanation of every bit of this example file. While the number of comments with dividing lines may seem an exaggeration, because this is a reduced demonstration file, you will not, at first glance, see any real benefits. But, in large files, such lines play an important role. When you're skimming through the code, they allow you to scroll faster, since you have a very distinct visual marker, very easy to spot even when scrolling at a relatively high speed. Thicker lines differentiate contexts in the file. Thinner lines split elements within those contexts. The "**EOF**" comment is used as a very verbose mark of where the end of the file is. Amongst other things, it helps to track down corrupted files and gives some sense of closure about the file, but is also useful when analyzing code printouts when you feel old school and want to use the pen.

The document header helps you track what you're doing, what you're editing, and who touched the file. If you need more detail about what every user did to the file, you can always check the logs of the version control system. But if you just need a quick reference, a "**CTRL+Home**" will give you that at any time. It is also important to credit the institution where this project is being developed. The dates are, in the case of the institution, the original creation date of the file and for the users, the date of the first time each user edited the file.

You undoubtedly noticed the usage of dual language comments. While working in a team composed of people with different nationalities, there are two different approaches you can use. You either define a pivot language and everyone must use that language in the comments, or you allow comments to be multilingual, like the strings of a multi-language software are. There are benefits in this approach for a very simple reason. By allowing more than one language, you are allowing people to add comments in the languages they know. They are supposed to add comments in a language they share with mostly everybody. In this case, Portuguese and English. Suppose you have an English speaking colleague and a Portuguese speaking one. The Portuguese speaking one does not master the English as well as you do. And the English guy does not understand Portuguese. However, you understand both languages. You can read the Portuguese comments your colleague added and fix his English comments or add them if he wasn't able to.

Adding to that, not only the two characters identifying the language, but the entire structure of the document, since it is based in well defined rules regarding spacing, lines and comments, it is easier for you to write some kind of information gathering system, if you wish to extract documentation directly from your code, as Doxygen does, without filling up the file with an immense amount of text that makes navigating through the file more difficult.

Another thing that makes no sense is to limit the width of the file to 80 characters. Nowadays, screens are wide and have enough resolution to hold way more than 80 characters. This allows a cleaner file by reducing the need of line breaks in strings and single statements. We are no longer in the era of the teletype terminal. And this is only one of the countless artificial limitations some of our contemporary developers still unknowingly apply due to historic reasons. This reminds of a story of about monkeys in the cage. Scientists were trying to understand violence within primates. So they had three monkeys locked in a cage with a banana hanging from the cage's ceiling. Whenever one monkey would attempt to steal the banana, the other two monkeys would be given a cold bath with a fire hose. With time, whenever any monkey would approach the banana, the other two would spank the poor bastard. Then, after a long period, they would replace one of the monkeys for another monkey that had never been in contact with the other monkeys. The poor soul would attempt to reach the banana and get spanked. At some point, all monkeys would have already been replaced, one at a time. However, the ritual spanking was still present, despite the fact that none of the monkeys then in the cage had ever been subjected to the cold bath. The situation described applies to a lot of our behavior today in computing, like, for example, having to support outdated legacy systems that slow down our progress.

After discussing the header files, which contain the declarations, now it's time to analyze the files that contain the actual statements, the ".c" or ".cpp" files. A ".cpp" file typically contains less different sections than the corresponding header file, since most of the declarations, if not all, have been placed in that header. Let's examine the ".cpp" file that complements the previous header example:

```
1
2   // source/folder/CObject.cpp – short description
3   // From package PackageName
4   // 2008+ The institution
5   // 2008+ First guy who worked on this file
6   // 2008+ Second guy who worked on this file
7
8   // ===========================================================
9   // PT: pré-processador
10  // EN: pre-processor
11  // ===========================================================
12
13  #include "MyProject.h"
14
15
16
17  // ===========================================================
18  // PT: início do código
19  // EN: code begins
20  // ===========================================================
21
22  // -----------------------------------------------------------
```

```
23  // PT: ampliar o objecto
24  // EN: zoom the object
25  bool CObject::zoom(float p_scale)
26  {
27    m_scale = p_scale;
28
29    return(true);
30  }
31
32
33  // ----------------------------------------------
34  // PT: mover o objecto
35  // EN: move the object
36  bool CObject::move(float p_x, float p_y, float p_z)
37  {
38    // PT: acertar os membros é suficiente
39    // EN: setting the members is enough
40    m_x = p_x;
41    m_y = p_y;
42    m_z = p_z;
43
44    // PT: retornar verdadeiro para ser redesenhado
45    // EN: return true to be redrawn
46    return(true);
47  }
48
49
50
51  // ==============================================
52  // === EOF ======================================
53  // ==============================================
54
```

As you can see, it's similar to the header file. The logic behind it still applies, dividing sections and subsections appropriately, maintaining consistency in the number of blank lines and spaces. Also, the amount of comments is reduced and the comments are kept simple. As said before, it is preferred to keep them simple and reduced because you may not want to bloat your code with too much text. You may be better off by writing short, simple comments that explain snippets or short blocks of code, and have self-documenting symbols and code, rather than explaining everything in detail. That's something you should leave for the low-level architecture document. Using the comments to provide references and parallelisms with the architecture documents is much more efficient.

3.4 Naming conventions

Part of the readability of code stems from the naming scheme applied when writing it. Having a good naming convention is an important step towards achieving that state. There are several well known naming conventions out there. Microsoft, for example, uses the Hungarian notation in their C and C++ APIs. The purpose of that naming convention was to be language independent and it was first used with the BCPL programming language. The reason for its use with BCPL was that the language had no data types besides the default machine word and, therefore, nothing in it could help the programmer remember the types. Hungarian notation provides a way to, from the name of the symbol, decipher its type. In BASIC, for example, the character present in the tail of the symbol name would identify its type, despite the fact that recent evolution cycles of that language have eliminated much of the use of such suffixes.

However, you'll learn, most of the times, it is harder, and more useful, to know where the symbol came from, and not as much the type, as that can be easily known either from the context or from the origin of the symbol. These code conventions, had a long time to evolve and have revealed themselves very useful, not only in providing a greater level of readability, but also in helping to make sure the number of mistakes resulting from naming confusions were greatly reduced, if not totally eliminated. The prefixes were carefully chosen to avoid any conflicts. But prefixes alone are not enough to make a good name. You need also to use your best judgment to come up with a simple yet descriptive name for your symbol. Out of pure fun, to have some kind of an easter egg embedded into the source, a team member of a certain project, added a variable with an incredibly appropriate name: "`m_stupidMicrosoftSpecificThingGodIHateThis`". Don't do that. Unless it's really, really funny.

> It is more important to know the origin of a symbol than the type.

Now, let's discuss about prefixes applied only to variables. It is important to understand variable origins. If you know where they came from, you can easily refer to the declaration if you forget the type. Most of the times, knowing where they are from is much more useful:

- "`p_`": variables prefixed with this element are parameters. Their only context is within the function or method inside which they are used.
- "`m_`": variables starting with this element are members of a class or structure.
- "`l_`": this element identifies local variables, valid only within the scope of a function.
- "`G_`": variables with this prefix are global variables. The reason for capitalizing the "`G`" in these is because they are located at the highest possible level where symbols

can be declared.

The following prefixes are used only to identify custom defined types:
- "`T`": identifies "typedefs".
- "`E`": identifies "exceptions".
- "`C`": identifies "classes".
- "`S`": identifies "structures".
- "`U`": identifies "unions".
- "`E_`": this is the only one to use the underscore in this category and stands for "enumerations".

Not included into any of the previous categories, "`_M_`" identifies macros. If you have members in a class, then you'll probably need "getter" and "setter" functions. It is a good policy to prefix those by either "`get_`" or "`set_`", followed by the exact same name of the member or property they refer to. In the end, namespaces are the only elements that receive a full non-prefixed name and everything else becomes easy to track. Also, there is, sometimes, the case of distinguishing public from private and protected methods. When such thing is necessary, a good way to do so is by using a single underscore as the prefix of the private and protected methods. It is not as important to tell a private from a protected method, but it is important to distinguish both of them from the public ones.

3.5 Mixing C and C++

You can mix C and C++. Despite what some people may think, it's not necessarily a bad thing. Actually, most times, it is the only way to get things done. Most current operating systems are built using pure C, as well as the great majority of frameworks and libraries. If your program is written in C++, this means you need to be able to link to the C libraries. You can also do the opposite, with some caveats.

3.5.1 Compiler requirements

To be as sure as possible that your cake tastes good, you need to use compilers from the same vendor, of compatible versions. Otherwise, you'll have no guarantee that the calling and naming conventions are compatible. It is also important that your "`main()`" function be compiled by the C++ compiler. This will make sure that the initialization of static elements is executed. Otherwise, you're in trouble. You must also allow the C++ compiler to be the one managing the linking. This way you can be sure it will include the necessary base libraries and initialization code.

3.5.2 Code specifics

When using the standard C library, be sure to use the new C++ headers. For example, instead of using "`stdio.h`", use "`cstdio`". In C, you would do this:

```
#include <stdio.h>
```

But in C++, you have to do:

```
#include <cstdio>
```

You will also need to change some habits, as in C you'd do this:

```
int i = getchar();
```

and with C++ you have to do this:

```
int i = std::getchar();
```

This happens because, with the new headers, the functions are inside the "**std**" namespace, which actually makes sense. However, this is only true for the standard library's headers. With third party headers, things might be different. If a library has not been planned with the possibility of C++ in mind, you will not find any headers explicitly prepared for C++.

Because C++ uses name mangling[8], the compiler will be expecting the C functions to have compatible names, with the appropriate prefixes and suffixes. But the C compiler doesn't use name mangling because C does not support overloading. For that reason, you'll be in trouble, unless you have a way to tell the C++ compiler that a specific function is a C function. And you do. By using the "**extern**" declaration, you can achieve such an effect:

```
extern "C"
```

---

8 *Name mangling is a technique, required for function and operator overloading, that adds a prefix and a suffix to the name of each individual function so they can all be present in the object file without collisions.*

```
{
  #include "someOtherHeader.h"
}
```

And, then, you can just go on about your life and use the functions you want. You can also apply the "extern" construct to isolated functions. Now, if you're developing your own C libraries, and you want them to be compatible with C++ directly, the compiler (and the preprocessor) are your friends. By using a special macro defined by the C++ compiler, you can make your headers very polite to both languages:

```
1  #ifdef __cplusplus
2  extern "C"
3  {
4  #endif
5  ...
6  // your code here
7  ...
8  #ifdef __cplusplus
9  }
10 #endif
```

It's pretty much self-explaining. The C++ compiler, and only the C++ compiler, not a C compiler, will define the "**__cplusplus**" macro. You can detect it and, inside both constructs, you can place the declaration of your functions.

The last two things you need to take into account are memory related, the first being about passing structures and the second about memory management. If you need to pass data structures, you must use structures that can be compiled by the pure C compiler, due to the hidden data that C++ structures get.

The last thing you need to take into account is memory. The C language doesn't have the operators "**new**" and "**delete**". If the C code you're calling is expected to release memory you reserved, be sure to reserve that memory block using "**malloc()**". Should you need to release memory allocated by a C function, then you'll have to use "**free()**". Refer to section 4.5 for more information on the subject.

4 Defensive programming

Defensive programming is a discipline on software design focused on the robustness of computing systems. The idea behind it is to develop the software in such a way that it dissolves or even eliminates the susceptibility of such a system to unforeseen circumstances, like attempts to circumvent or deliberately misuse such software, or environmental causes. In other words, nobody wants Murphy's Law[9] to be called into scene. As said in the introduction, this book is mainly about

---

9 *If anything can go wrong, it probably will.*

defensive programming. This section, however, focuses more on the code bits.

4.1 Code reuse

> Give preference to code reuse over reinventing the wheel.

One of the first rules you need to learn is that code reuse **is a good thing**. The more a particular piece of code is used, the better it becomes. It undergoes more testing, in different situations. And it matures with testing. This means that your product's dependencies will be more reliable. This also means that you'll have less work, because if you're reusing code, there's less coding you need to actually do. This implies that you will need to use libraries to share and isolate your code. Google has an interesting internal policy regarding code. All produced code is available to everyone inside the company so that they don't have to reinvent, or, in this case, rewrite, the wheel. There are disadvantages, of course. With this policy, it is impossible to compartmentalize information, specifically code, and, theoretically, at least, it is much harder to prevent leaks. Theoretically, because, if you look through history, Microsoft, a company with much tighter policies when it comes to compartmentalizing information, has suffered, according to the press and for a number of different reasons, much harder hits. For several times, the press announced Microsoft had suffered a code leak, while it was tried, it was impossible to find a single reference to Google suffering a leak, even after searching for that on Bing. Perhaps Google's internal openness makes employees less interested in sabotaging by exposing company secrets, perhaps it's just a matter of different quality in security measures or just coincidence.

It matters, therefore, that you learn how to use libraries, how to link them to your program and how to build your own. Methods for building libraries vary greatly from platform to platform but each platform has specific tools and very useful documentation on how to proceed. You need to pay attention to where you place the libraries so that you can be sure that the code, or the operating system where the code is running, can find them. You might also want to explore a similar system to the one Google uses. It might be interesting to have, in your company's intranet, a browsable and searchable repository of generic code snippets that can be used off-the-shelf, when libraries are not appropriate. But more than that, a centralized and properly organized library of documentation and information is imperative.

Due to its nature and object oriented features, C++ is a language that allows, improves and actively enables code reuse. Templates and inheritance contribute to such endeavor and C++ takes it further by allowing multiple inheritance, a feature which even most of the more complete object oriented languages lack.

4.2 Preprocessor

The preprocessor is a very powerful tool for developers if correctly used. Many languages support some form of preprocessor embedded into their full compiler suite. For some other languages, there are external preprocessors that are called independently from the language compiler to preprocess the source code. The C (and C++) preprocessor, however, is especially evolved and feature packed. The main features are the same for all available compilers, since they're standardized, but there are also some specific characteristics and functionalities that vary from one to another. Learning to dominate the preprocessor brings additional weapons and possibilities.

4.2.1 Conditional compilation

This is a technique that allows the programmer, at compile time, to tell the compiler which path to choose from a series of possible ones. With this technique, three important possibilities become immediately notorious:
1. The fact that it eases the construction of portable software, by providing the compiler with different snippets of code for the specific characteristics of the platforms. By checking predefined macros, the compiler is able to determine which of the snippets is the correct one for the selected platform.
2. New possibilities for debugging without the need to constantly rewrite code while testing it.
3. The ability to select, at compile time, which features will be available on your product.

4.2.1.1 Portability and feature selection

Conditional compilation is often achieved by using the "#if", "#ifdef" and "#ifndef" directives (and derivatives like "#else", "#elif", etc). It can also be achieved by simply defining macros and carefully placing them. You might use something like the following example to allow a specific part of your project to compile both under Windows and Linux:

```
1  #ifdef __WINDOWS__
2  ...
3  // specific Windows code
4  ...
5  #elif defined(__LINUX__)
6  ...
7  // specific Linux source
8  ...
9  #endif
```

This, of course, implies that everything is correctly built in order to make sure that the macros "__WINDOWS__" and "__LINUX__" are mutually exclusive and can't be defined simultaneously. If, for some reason, they are not mutually exclusive in definition, there is code that can cause severe problems. If (most likely, because of a programmer error) both macros end up being defined, the following code will ruin your day:

```
1  ...
2  // code
3  ...
4
5  #ifdef __LINUX__
6  ...
7  /*
8     code for an extra step that is needed under
9     Linux but not under Windows
10 */
11 ...
12 #endif
13
14 ...
15 // more code
```

```
16 ...
```

Since both macros are defined, the compiler will, for conditional blocks based on "`#ifdef-#else`" use just the code for the first macro found, in this case, the "`__WINDOWS__`" macro. However, in this example, if both macros are defined, on the "`#ifdef-#else`" blocks, the Windows specific code will be selected. But, in blocks like this one, where the block itself presents no means for mutual exclusion, and because "`__LINUX__`" is also defined, the Linux code will also be compiled and you're doomed to hell.

There are a few ways to help you avoid this problem. The first one is by you becoming a sacred programmer from Olimpus, that never makes any mistake and has the uncanny ability to write operating systems from scratch using "`cat > source.asm`". Better still, if you develop the ability to directly reprogram your computer by shaking a magnetized needle over the motherboard bus, perfect. If you can do that, then, you might be good enough to never make any mistakes and never have your supposedly mutual exclusive macros defined at the same time. And even then it's uncertain. The alternative is using one of the other realistic ways to do this.

One way is to never leave isolated conditional blocks that depend on macros mutually exclusive sets, like the one presented above. If you have no code for the blocks corresponding to other macros, then leave them empty. It won't do any harm, it will not make it more difficult to read the code, it will work perfectly and, if in the future you need to add specific code for any other macros, you just need to fill in the blanks.

Many projects usually have one major header file where you, or your team, are placing generic data, macros, definitions and information that needs to be available to all compilable source files in it. Such file is, most of the times, generated dynamically during the compilation process, being always one of the first compilable files to be created. Usually, this is a file called "`config.h`", which contains all the static data. It is also frequent to have a "`platform.h`" file in multi-platform projects, where platform specific information is placed. If you can figure out a way that such mutually exclusive macros are generated automatically and placed in one of those files, so that mutual exclusion is assured, then you can go about your day.

There is also a safe alternative, which is to play with the preprocessor once again. You can make sure that only one of the macros is defined:

```
1  #ifdef __WINDOWS__
2  #undef __LINUX__
3  #endif
```

This snippet makes sure that the macros can't be defined simultaneously, since it will void the concurrent macro. This will work, of course, unless some other preprocessor code further in redefines the previously undefined macro. In this specific case, since the example is related to platform specific code, it is a good idea to include such code in the "`platform.h`" file. It is left as an exercise to the reader to figure out how to proceed, should there be more than two target platforms on the project. Be advised that many development kits already come packed with features to help you deal with specificities of platforms. You should first refer to the appropriate documentation for those development kits. Also, be aware of the following two aspects: first, making a product multi-platform is not the only situation you'll find that requires mutually exclusive conditional compilation – it will be up to you to find out where to place the exclusion code – and second, sometimes you will need to use mutual exclusion macros in an inclusive manner. You will need to enable compilation for code that has to be available to more than one compilation path. There is also the case of code that requires that more than one macro to be defined. In summary, there is no universal solution. You must know what to apply based on your needs.

4.2.1.2 Preprocessor assisted debugging

Conditional compilation also plays an important role in the debugging of your program. If it is well structured, your project will, with no doubt, have at least two compilation modes. One called "debug" and another called "release". When in debug mode, you will need your program to perform some additional tasks, strictly for debugging purposes, like outputting information on some specific points of execution (tracing) or to ensure your software simply quits, should some predefined condition in your code fail to be met (assertions). You surely do not want your project outputting trace information or evaluating the assertion conditions when it has been finally deployed on a client. It is preferable not to have such code in the release version because it increases the binary size, slows down execution and it is likely to fill the client's screen with a ton of information he may not be able to understand and probably doesn't interest him at all.

The standard C library provides you with the "`assert()`" macro. Such a macro will allow you to make sure that your program, at specified points, will either meet a condition or die. It is a valuable tool for any programmer while attempting to debug the code and to help him make sure the code does what it is supposed to:

```
assert( i != 0 );
```

This macro takes one argument, an expression, which must be possible to evaluate to a boolean (actually, to any C POD data type value). Should the expression evaluate to false or null, "`assert()`" calls "`abort()`", killing the process and printing text with information similar to the following:

```
assert: file.c:10:main: Assertion 'i != 0' failed.
```

Assertions are especially valuable in helping you find the most strange and unimaginable types of bugs, things that seem not to make any sense and even hardware failures. However, you need to be careful about something commonly referred to as "Heisenbugs". Heisenberg's principle of uncertainty states that you are unable to accurately measure a property of an object being studied without either affecting such property or a complimentary one. Why is this relevant? Because of the way "`assert()`" works. Take a look at the following simplified implementation of "`assert()`", while not exactly the most complete, it will do for this explanation:

```
1  #ifdef NDEBUG
2  #define assert(condition) (void(0))
3  #else
4  #define assert(condition) ... /* assert code */
5  #endif
```

In this case, if the "**NDEBUG**" macro (which means "no debug") is defined, the "**assert()**" macro will evaluate to an empty statement. But, if the macro is not defined, then your assertion will evaluate into compilable code that will run. This is where the "heisenbugs" come from. While it is desirable that debug code does not exist in a release version of the project, it is important that, functionally-wise, both versions are as similar as possible. If you have any kind of function call, control statement or data-altering statement inside the assertion, that code will exist only in the debug version, leaving you with potentially critical different results between the release and debug versions. Basically, you will be introducing a bug.

Another important macro that may be either part of your compiler's base library or any framework you're using, is the "**TRACE(x, ...)**" macro. This macro works, in most implementations, in a similar fashion to "**printf(const char *, ...)**", receiving a format string and a list of parameters in the order they appear in the format list. By using that macro you can, in specific points in code, output important debug information. It's called "**TRACE()**" because it allows you to trace program execution and variable values based on the specific information you require. The same way as with "**assert()**", the "**TRACE()**" macro will be graciously ignored if the project is compiled in release mode.

4.2.1.3 Macros

While preprocessor macros can be an invaluable tool for a lot of situations, you may want to be careful with what you use them for. The advice of being careful with your choices and using the best judgment to decide what to use, and when, can't be stressed enough. For that, here are some important tips. If you've done a lot of C coding, and if you're used to the C standard library, then you're more than likely used to the application of macros. They allow you to hide values and pieces of code under a meaningful name, reducing your need to explicitly repeat those values and snippets throughout your project.

The C++ language, and some recent (and others not so recent) changes to C introduced several new schemes you can use to avoid using macros. For instance, you may be used to do something like the following code to give a symbolic name to a certain value:

```
#define PI_APPROX 3.141593
```

Then you use that symbol in your code, but forget that macros are for the preprocessor's eyes only. Once the preprocessor does its job, the compiler will see no macro name, only the value. Now suppose that, somewhere along the code, there is some kind of an error. If that value was involved, the compiler would not print the name "**PI_APPROX**", but rather the value 3.141593. You immediately know what that value is and that is helpful in finding out the problem. But, if the value was something else with no meaning to you, you'd have no way to find out what it was immediately, unless you'd enlist the help of good old "`grep`". It is true that the compiler gives you a line number with the error and you can check out what's written in that line. But what if the line had more than one macro? And what if the error is reported not by the compiler, but by an assertion in a library to which you have no access to the code? **In that case, the solution is to either use constants or enumerations.** It is common for the "`assert()`" macro to also print out the line that caused the assertion to fail. This means that you will be able to see which symbols were involved in that failure. Also, because the constant and enumeration names are entered into the compiler's symbol table during compilation, the message will bear more meaning to you.

> Prefer constants and enumerations to macros.

The situation becomes harder when constant pointers are in the way. It is the situation you will face when dealing with null terminated strings. If you're lucky, some compilers will have only one copy compiled into the program. Some other will have as many as referenced. But you're likely to be unable to do whatever you want to that string. You're better off transforming it into a constant pointer to a constant string. And, when dealing with any kind of constants, you may want to maintain some structure and to declare your constants within a certain context. Some of them can and should actually be declared in specific classes. You will face many situations where your constants are only useful inside one particular class or with that particular class and, therefore, you can actually declare those constants in the class, likely as a static constant. Now, much of the same applies to code macros, but for that you should refer to section 4.7.2, where inline functions are explained in more detail.

4.2.2 Compilation process debugging

In some situations, you will need to gain a better understanding of what your compiler is doing. Sometimes you need to debug preprocessor macros you wrote. Debugging those is frequently a tedious and difficult task. One of the reasons is that macros are evaluated in compile time, implying that you need to recompile your project each time you want to check them. It is different with code, because usually you can perform a lot of debugging and testing from a single run of a compilation. The majority of programs have a long run or a continuous cycle. This allows you to evaluate several aspects of the project at once. As for the compilation process, you are not that lucky. You have one single run from which to extract valuable information.

You can use some special directives to help you generate a trace of how the compiler is interpreting them. Most of these directives can vary from compiler to compiler, but one is always present: "**#error**", which prints out a message of your choosing and forces the compiler to abort compilation. This error directive is also useful when you want to prevent someone from including an header directly due to dependencies. Suppose you want the header "**b.h**" to only be included by header "**a.h**" and never by the user. A construct as simple as the following would do the trick:

File "**a.h**":

```
1  #ifndef __A_H__
2  #define __A_H__
```

```
3   ...
4   #include "b.h"
5   ...
6   #endif
```

File "`b.h`":

```
1   #ifndef __A_H__
2   #error "This header can only be included from a.h"
3   #endif
4   ...
```

As you can see, the "`#error`" directive can easily be placed along the code, if you want to understand what the compiler is doing with your macros. It is a safe and effective way to debug the compilation process. And, in some cases, you can also use the macros "`#warning`" or "`#pragma message`", depending on the compiler, if you do not wish the compilation process to be aborted.

4.2.3 Obsolescence

When you are phasing out features on your project, particularly API features, like headers or functions, it would be nice to have a way to warn the users of your API that they will eventually be removed, while not removing such features immediately. This would allow the developer some time to slowly adapt his projects. Including such information in the documentation is imperative, but it should come as no surprise that documentation, for a developer, is usually the first thing to be bypassed because of a natural tendency developers have to do things by heart or intuition. By using the preprocessor's compile-time messaging features, you are able to do it in a non disruptive, yet sufficiently, intrusive way to ensure that the users of your API are made aware of it as much as possible. Depending on the compiler, you may be able to use the directives "**#warning**", "**#pragma message**" or even "**#obsolete**" and "**#deprecated**". Should portability between compilers be required, you will need to come up with a mechanism to ensure that, despite the compiler, the user will be warned of such obsolescence. If the phase out period is nearing its end, you may want to let the user of your product know that it is his last chance to use that specific obsolete feature. In such case, the best thing to do may be to force the developer to confirm his need to use such a feature in a preemptive way. One simple way to do so, is to use a mechanism such as:

```
1  #ifndef _I_AM_REALLY_SURE_
2  #error "Obsolete feature. Are you sure you want it?"
3  #endif
4  #warning "Fire will fall from the skies..."
5  ... // feature defined here
6  #endif
```

This can be applied to a header you want to phase out. This way the developer is forced to define the macro "**_I_AM_REALLY_SURE_**", otherwise, the code will not compile. If he screws up now, it's his fault. You are supposed to be a good programmer, but you can't be expected to save the world and save everybody from themselves. Sometimes, professional darwinism should be applied to developers.

4.3 Variables

Every program element is susceptible to it's own pitfalls and variables are not an exception. There is a lot to say about variables, justifying a whole section about them.

4.3.1 Comparisons and assignments

As you probably should know (and if you don't, then it's suggested you study the language a bit more, at first), the assignment operator ("`=`") works like a function, taking two operands and returning a value. Consider three variables called "`result`", "`lhs`" (for left hand side), and "`rhs`" (for right hand side). Suppose, if you like, they are all integers. And now, take the sum operator ("`+`"), for example. You use it like this:

```
result = lhs + rhs;
```

The sum operator takes "`lhs`" and "`rhs`", adds them together, and places the result on "`result`". None of the operands suffers any change, only the "`result`" variable does. The assignment operator works similarly. However, in an assignment, one of the operands is changed: the left hand side operand receives the value of the right hand side. Since an assignment is an expression just like any other, it must be possible to evaluate it to a value. In the sum operation, the compiler evaluates it to the sum of the operands, in the assignment operation, the compiler evaluates it to the value of the right hand side. That allows you to do something like this:

```
1  result = lhs = rhs;
2
3  result = (lhs = rhs);
```

In C and C++ code, you can do something like that. You can daisy chain assignments so that all variables in the chain have the same final value. This is because each assignment is a separate operation and those are evaluated from right to left. The final value of "**result**", in any of the presented cases is the value of "**rhs**".

It important to know this, because a simple typo can really ruin your day. The identity relational operator, "**==**", is only one single character away from you messing up your code due to a typing error. All control statements in C and C++ accept any expression that returns a POD[10] value as a condition. And since any function call that returns a value (therefore, void functions are excluded) is a valid expression then, unless you find a way to go around this, you're pretty much asking for trouble. Conditional statements like, for example, "**if**" and "**while**", don't really care what the type returned from an expression is as long as they can evaluate it to zero or anything else. Consider the following example:

```
1  if(var_a == 2) { /* do something */ }
2  if(var_a = 2) { /* do something */ }
```

If you wanted to have something like what you have on line 1, but, because of a typo, you end up writing what's on line 2,

---

10 *Plain Old Data - any of the basic built-in or primitive data types (integers, floats, characters, pointers and booleans)*

the compiler will accept it also. After all, it is a valid expression and returns a value the "`if`" statement can evaluate. And just like that you've wrecked your code and it is likely that, when the bug surfaces, you'll likely take a long time spotting it. You can avoid this problem with a very simple trick that you must force yourself to always apply. As you know, you can't assign values to just any kind of element. Just to variables. So, it is enough to reverse the order of the members in the expression and the compiler will automatically trigger an error, should you mistype the operator:

> Becoming self-disciplined is an imperative step in producing good code.

```
1  if(2 == var) { /* do something */ } // correct
2  if(2 = var)  { /* do something */ } // error
```

Reversing the order will not change how the program behaves but will, however, change how the compiler behaves. The compiler will detect your mistake and will issue an error in accordance. You would be able to immediately spot the typo and fix it. It is a healthy habit to always write, in relational expressions, the read-only element on the left hand side of the operator and the writable element on the right-hand side. Beware that some compilers do warn you (probably depending on the command-line options) about having assignments in place of expressions with a boolean result. To tell the compiler to STFU, you just need to do this:

```
if((var = 2)) { /* do something */ } //
```

But it is still better to use the previous method, as it will always work and provide you with the best result. As said before, good programming is about discipline. Now, what if both the left hand side and right hand side of the relational operator were valid writable expressions? Or if they both were variables that you needed to compare? In that case, it is a good idea to pay a big deal of attention to what you are doing. If you really need to setup a habit for extremely hardcore fail-proof coding practices, there are a few things you can try, but many of them may not be worth it. First, you can setup an "**inline**" function that returns the value of the variable. Example for integers:

```
inline int retintval(int p_value) { return(p_value) };
```

You could then use it in a comparison like the following:

```
if(retintval(var_a) == var_b) { /* do something */ };
```

Since "**retintval()**" is an inline function, for this specific case, the generated binary code will be the same as if you never used it in the first place. The compiler is intelligent enough to do so. And the execution will be the same. However, the compiler has more work to do and more information on how to process what you want the program to do. And we come back to the errors the compiler will issue should you mistype the operator.

There is one last situation you need to be aware of. Remember that C++ has references. At first glance, the expression "`func() = 10;`" might not seem to make sense, however, if your function returns a reference for an integer, for example, or any other type with "`operator=()`" defined, then the code will actually be valid. This means that, when using a function returning references, the condition evaluation statements will still be susceptible to the same problem explained before.

4.3.2 Variable misuse

While variables declared but not used usually[11] don't pose a risk to your program other than spending unneeded memory (and even that is undesirable), **variables improperly declared, without being initialized, pose a serious threat.** Never, ever, forget to initialize your variables. Uninitialized variables will present you with situations of undefined behavior and inconsistent behavior across platforms. The last thing you want is unpredictability.

> Don't forget to initialize variables.

Another problem you may find nowadays is related to strings. If you have strings declared in your code, in a lot of modern compilers, that data ends up in the read only section of memory. Do not try to overwrite them. If you need to manipulate those strings, copy them to a dynamically allocated block of memory and treat the originals as constants. Read

---

11 *I wrote "usually" because a declared but unused variable, if left in a structure, class, or even in the global pool or stack, and you attempt to play with pointers and lower level programming, it may still get in the way.*

section 4.3.4 for more information.

You may also want to take some care with the chronology of variable declaration. In C you would declare variables at the beginning of a function. In C++, you don't need to do the same and, actually, it may be better if you don't. **Try to declare variables only near the point where you first need them.** There's the exception of dealing with loops. In that case you may be interested in paying attention to section 6.2.2.

> Declare variables when you need them.

4.3.3 Pointer arithmetic problems

Pointer arithmetic can give you a headache. Be careful with it, as you may end up either overwriting data you need or touching protected memory and having your program blow up in your face. Beware of the increment ("**++**") and decrement ("**--**") operators when applied to pointers, as they increment the pointers not in single byte units, but in the size of the element they point to. For instance, if you have a pointer to a character, the increment operator will increment the pointer by one. But if you have a pointer to a short integer, the operator will increment it by two. Basically, when talking about pointers, the increment operator is equivalent to adding "`sizeof(*pointer_var)`" to the pointer. The equivalent is also true for the decrement operator. Remember this so you don't fall into your own traps.

4.3.4 String constants

You should beware of string constants. While, in "the old days", you could write to the space they occupied as if it was any piece of heap space, today, you better not. Even then it was a bad practice and it is still worse today. Most modern compilers put data in read-only sections of memory, sometimes packed up with the code. That means you'll be most likely setting your process on fire by triggering an exception when trying to access a memory location in a way you're not allowed to. **The smart thing to do, when playing with string constants, is to copy them to the heap** if you know you'll need to modify them in any way or if they need to be available to functions you do not know.

> Copy your string constants to the heap.

4.3.5 Casts

Casts are important, but they, too, have their drawbacks. For your own protection and probably better readability of the code, you should use the new C++ types of cast. The C-style casts are dangerous because they let you cast mostly everything to anything. They do no checking, whatsoever. With C++ casts, on the other hand, you are in a much better situation. For instance, if you're casting down in the derivation hierarchy of a class, in the case of using pointers, you'll get a null pointer should the cast fail. If you're casting references, you'll get an exception. Either way, you have the possibility to know if cast worked. C++ casts are more strict. They help you protect your program from failure. You have four cast types in C++. The "`static_cast`" is pretty much the same thing as the old C-style cast. The "`dynamic_cast`" allows you to cast within the inheritance hierarchy of a set of classes. The "`const_cast`" allows you to manipulate the "`const`" and "`volatile`" attributes of an element. And then you have the "`reinterpret_cast`", when you need to perform a cast unrelated to inheritance. However, beware that this last type of cast usually produces code that is non-portable.

4.4 Compiler messages

Sometimes, people don't realize they can have the compiler working for them in more ways than they imagine. **Specifically, they can have the compiler help them detecting errors that might otherwise go unnoticed.** Take, for example, the situation with comparisons presented in section 4.3.1. This, of course, implies that

> Have the compiler work for you.

you develop some discipline, as with everything else. It goes without saying that you should pay close attention to the messages produced by the compiler. Not only the error messages, but also the warning messages. All of them contain important information that you'll need to learn to interpret. Since both the codes and messages for errors and warnings are different from compiler to compiler, it isn't possible to present you a detailed description on them and on how to interpret them. However, some generic tips on the most common compiler messages and some tips related to the situations when the solution is not as obvious as it first seems, can be found in this section. These are based on GCC's version of the messages, but equivalent messages can be obtained with compilers from other vendors.

4.4.1 Errors

4.4.1.1 Undeclared identifier

This message doesn't always mean the identifier hasn't been declared. Sometimes it is actually missing but, in many other situations, the problem is different. An "undeclared identifier" message can be triggered by reasons such as these:
- The identifier isn't actually there - either it never existed or there is a typo in the declaration of the symbol or in the place where it was used;
- The identifier has been declared, but is inaccessible from the current scope - this usually happens if the identifier has been declared on a different scope, but you failed to refer to the scope containing it;
- The identifier was declared in an header file you forgot to include;
- None of the above is true, which means you are calling the right scope, you have the right headers, but because of some preprocessor magic and conditional compilation macros, your symbol isn't visible anyway;
- Your compiler is broken.

So, take the previous list as a checklist and, whenever you find yourself in such situation, verify your project item by item. The order may not be the most appropriate, but that will depend on the nature of your project.

4.4.1.2 Functions are abstract

You cannot instantiate an abstract class. If it is abstract, not all methods are implemented. Therefore, if you try to create an object from an abstract class, you'll be stopped by the compiler with a message such as this:

```
test.cpp: In function 'int main()':
test.cpp:8: error: cannot allocate an object of
abstract type 'CTest'
test.cpp:2: note:   because the following virtual
functions are pure within 'CTest':
test.cpp:3: note:   virtual void CTest::func()
```

If you weren't expecting this message, confirm that all the members of your class are implemented. If the class inherits from another, check the ancestor class or classes recursively for members that were supposed to be implemented in the derived classes.

4.4.1.3 Undefined reference

This is the kind of error you will get during the linking stage, and not actually during compilation. It usually means that you failed to include a module or a library you were supposed to. Sometimes, however, it is a bit tricker. It can be the result of a method you declared in the prototype of a class but forgot to implement. If everything is correctly implemented in your class, check the ancestor classes as well.

4.4.1.4 Undefined reference to 'main'

This is a special case of the previous error. You may have forgotten to include a "`main()`" function in your code. If that's not the problem, that only means you did not want a "`main()`" function at all, because the module you were trying to compile wasn't supposed to produce an executable alone, and forgot to use the correct compiler switches. When you're compiling single modules and do not wish an executable to be produced right away, you should instruct your compiler to produce just the object file. In GCC, for example, you can do so with the option "-c" added to the command-line.

4.4.2 Warnings

4.4.2.1 Comparison between signed and unsigned

If you attempt to compare elements of different sign attributes, like comparing a variable of unsigned type with a variable of signed type, you'll be facing one of these messages. You need to be vary careful about this situation because of the way signed and unsigned numbers are stored in memory. When comparing both, if the value in the signed int is negative, you may be getting the wrong result from the comparison. Investigate further about how integer values are stored in memory for more details on why this is such a bad idea.

4.4.2.2 Member initializers will be reordered

In section 5.2.2.1, it is explained why it is a good idea to have the initialization of your members in the same order as they are declared in the class prototype. If your compiler is smart and in the mood to save you some work, instead of just telling you that you should reorder the initialization of your elements, it will reorder the elements during compilation. Check that section for more information.

4.4.2.3 Suggest parenthesis around assignment

Because of reasons explained in section 4.3.1, if your compiler is set to produce a sufficiently verbose message output, you'll be warned when you try to execute an assignment inside a control statement like "`if`".

```
test.cpp: In function `int main()':
test.cpp:30: warning: suggest parentheses around
assignment used as truth value
```

If you don't really want the compiler to complain and you are absolutely sure you want to perform that assignment inside the "`if`", just enclose your assignment with an extra pair of parentheses and you'll be set.

4.4.3 Special case: function warnings

Besides the language analysis related warnings, today's compilers are also prepared to issue additional information about some of the most common functions from the standard library. Those warnings are explained in a section ahead. These are some of the most notable ones:

- The "`gets()`" function - the compiler will warn you if you use this function as it is considered dangerous. Refer to section 4.7.6.1.
- The "`printf()`" family of functions – the compiler pays attention to the format identifiers used in the format string as well as the types passed and will match them against the format string.
- The "`mktemp()`", "`tempnam()`" and "`tmpnam()`"

functions are also susceptible to compiler warnings, due to the race conditions explained in section 4.8.

4.5 Memory management

Memory management, without question, is one of the most painful Achilles heels of software development, more so in languages like C and C++, where such management has to be fully handled by the developer. There is an extensive list of possible problems a project can suffer related to this subject. All of them are quite important and deserve special treatment. Userspace memory management has evolved a lot with the introduction of the protected mode in the PC platform. Most CPU architectures have some sort of MMU that provides memory space and process isolation. In the days of the original PC, although it was possible to have some rudimentary forms of multitasking, software was mostly based around a single process that took almost complete possession of the machine's resources. In terms of memory management, software had to take into account much more elements than today. Hardware access was easier and much more direct, for example. Also, some memory areas, although they allowed writing, were areas that weren't supposed to be used as general access memory, because they contained important information required either by the operating system or the BIOS and CPU. Therefore, memory access libraries, had to be written to take into account those details. With today's hardware based memory protection mechanisms, that's easier to deal with. Userspace memory management libraries today are simpler and have less external information to depend on.

4.5.1 Allocation

In C, you have available four functions to deal with dynamic memory allocation. You have two functions to allocate memory ("`malloc()`" and "`calloc()`", one to free it ("`free()`"), and other somewhere in between ("`realloc()`"). It is common to forget to check whether memory allocation has succeeded. The return value of the "`malloc()`" and "`calloc()`", as well as "`realloc()`" functions is "`NULL`" if they fail to reserve memory. However, because "`realloc()`" is used to resize a block of memory, it is common to find something like this:

```
myblock = realloc(myblock, newsize);
```

The problem with that code is the assumption that "`realloc()`" will not fail. That assumption is, unfortunately, common practice. The same holds true for the other functions. However, this code, in case of a failure, ends up producing yet more problems. Not only you fail to resize the block, but you'll also lose the pointer to the old, still valid block, because, when "`realloc()`" fails, it doesn't destroy the previous block.

Another common rookie (and sometimes not so rookie) mistake often found in C++ programming is based around the new facilities the language provides to deal with memory allocation. It is frequent to find situations where memory allocation has been done using "`malloc()`" or any of the base C standard library functions, but the release is attempted using "`delete`". The reverse is also common, finding allocations using "`new`" and a release using "`free()`". Sometimes, these problems are hard to debug, because the usage of the functions seems perfectly legitimate and, in many situations, they don't even seem to produce any palpable error or failure. However, it is important to use the proper combinations. Using "`delete`" to cleanup after "`new`" is important because "`delete`" takes care of object destruction, something that "`free()`" does not, since "`delete`" is a C++ statement and "`free()`" is a function intended for C. The reverse is also true. **Synchronism between allocation method choices must always be maintained.**

> Maintain synchronism between allocation methods.

One more detail you will probably want to consider is what to do after releasing a block of memory. Despite the fact that you released the block, the variable that held the pointer to it will still hold it, even though it is now invalid. Should the variable be submitted to posterior processing, there should be a way to mark that the pointer in that variable has been voided. The best way to do it is to set it to zero or "`NULL`". Both "`free()`" and "`delete`" will ignore null pointers safely, which simplifies your code, especially when your pointer variables are subject to processing posterior to the memory release. However, sometimes, it is possible to find code like this:

```
TMyStructure & l_structure = * new TMyStructure;
```

Although this may be useful for readability purposes, you need to take into account that when the function or method where the structure allocation was performed returns, the memory will not be released automatically, since the structure was reserved on the heap and not on the stack. That means that before leaving the function, your code will have to do the following:

```
delete & l_structure;
```

However, here you will have no chance of zeroing the reference. You will have to take care of your pointers and references. You must also know that it is not enough to guarantee synchronism between "**new**" and "**delete**" and "**malloc()**" and "**free()**". When dealing with arrays, you also have to make sure you have consistency between "**new[]**" and "**delete[]**", regardless of the type of the elements in the array. If you don't, you're likely incurring in the same problems: memory corruption and process termination.

4.5.2 Leaks

Memory leaks are, probably, the most common memory related problem found. They happen when allocated memory is not released when it ceases to be useful. It is a sad consequence of leaving all the memory management work to the hands of the programmer, who, not infallible, frequently overlooks certain situations. It is easy to lose track of memory by overwriting pointers. **One common source of memory leaks are incorrectly written destructors in the classes.** As the program runs, it keeps accumulating pieces of reserved, but inaccessible memory and, eventually, runs out of address space. The consequences are inevitable.

> Incorrectly written destructors are a common source of memory leaks.

Therefore, you need to track your memory and, if possible, come up with some sort of methodical routine that allows you to automate memory management. To help you with finding memory leaks during the debug process of your program, there are several tools. One such tool is "`valgrind`", which you should learn to use.

4.5.3 Cleanup

One common source of malicious attacks is through analysis of the information remnant in memory from a previous (or possibly current) process. It does not involve breaking memory protection mechanisms, but rather reading newly allocated memory. Imagine this situation:
- process A runs and asks for memory, filling it up with data;
- later, process A releases that block of memory;
- malicious process B asks for memory and ends up being given the memory block that process A released;
- malicious process B can now explore the contents, since neither the operating system or the CPU perform any cleanup of the memory a process releases.

To prevent such situation, you are highly encouraged to perform some sort of clean up on the memory block you're about to release. You can do so by either using the "`bzero()`" function, which, has been deprecated, or the "`memset()`" function. There is, however, a compromise to be made

> Beware of the information you leave lingering in memory, perform the necessary clean-ups

in this regard, as cleaning up memory implies that additional processing has to be done. Sometimes you'll disregard everything, sometimes you'll want to be selective about which memory releases are followed by a cleanup and, sometimes, you'll want to always clear the memory contents. It is up to you to determine which policy to apply. Nevertheless, the memory you are about to release isn't the only memory that you may wish to clean. It is frequently useful to clear memory you've just allocated and haven't used yet, as that would be the block equivalent of initializing a variable.

4.5.4 Suicidal objects

Although not common practice and not always advisable, it is possible for an object to kill itself - basically, doing "`delete this;`". To be able to pull this off, you need to be careful and make sure that a few conditions are met, so that it doesn't blow up on your face. Some of those conditions are usually hard to impose. Most of them become pretty obvious when explained. For instance, no other part of the method, or any other function it calls, can make any use of the "`this`" pointer after the instruction that deletes the object. This is only natural because, after deleting the object, the pointer becomes invalid. You cannot, also, allow it to access any other member of the object. You must also guarantee that the method that commits suicide is the last one to be called on the "`this`" pointer. And you can never commit suicide on an object that was not allocated by "`new`". It cannot be an object on the stack, a member of an array created by "`new[]`" nor an object initialized in a previously allocated

> Be very careful about suicidal objects.

memory area (the "placement new" semantics).

4.5.5 Placement new

This is a special use case of the "**new**" operator, that allows you to initialize an object in a previously allocated block of memory. It is not advisable practice. Its real world use cases are usually limited to low level programming, when it is necessary to map an object to a specific memory address so it can access some kind of hardware data. Take a look at the following piece of code that supposedly accesses the previously loaded master boot record[12] data, for a 16-bit real mode operating system loader:

```
1  // alignment has to be to the byte
2  // check sections 6.2.1.2 and 6.2.1.3
3  #pragma pack(push, 1)
4  // this structure is a simplified version of an MBR
5  typedef struct
6  {
7    char m_code[440];
8    char m_disksig[4];
9    char m_nulls[2];
10   char m_partitions[64];
11   char m_mbrsig[2];
12 } TMBR;
13 #pragma pack(pop)
14
15 // this is the actual address where the BIOS
16 // loads the MBR
17 void * l_mbrptr = 0x7C00;
18
19 // creating an object of type TMBR at the address
```

---

12 *The MBR (Master Boot Record) is the first sector of a hard disk, which contains the initial system boot code and partition layout information.*

```
20  TMBR * l_mbr = new(l_mbrptr) TMBR;
```

Of course, in this case, being such a trivial example with a simple structure, you could just as easily use a cast on the "`l_mbrptr`" variable. However, you could be using a more complex class, with methods and constructor without any further code change except for the structure declaration, as long as there were no virtual methods on the class. This allows you not only to build the object where you want it, but also to have its constructor called. If you use any virtual methods, your class will have hidden data, required to handle the run-time method resolution, and that will either void your ability to use this method or force you to use complicated and non-portable tricks to deal with the overhead of the hidden data.

4.6 User input

Whenever your code is expecting user input in any way, **you may want to (and this means <u>you must</u>) test the user input.** Even if the user is not trying to, there are tons of ways he can subvert and compromise the stability of your program. The simplest numeric input can take your life upside down if you let the cruel nullity blow up your division in your face. You must be prepared to deal with unexpected values, unexpected mouse clicks, invalid data formats, invalid file formats, non-existing files and a myriad of other potentially lethal problems which will haunt you during all your professional life. A common source of security problems is the famous "SQL Injection". Someone with sufficient knowledge

> Always test user input.

Edition Zero - Defensive programming

would manipulate a string input to an application or a webpage field, in such a way as to contain SQL code that would be executed on the server and either destroy, corrupt or retrieve supposedly confidential and protected data. In case you're using C++, you'll most likely be using a feature called "prepared statements", which will help you prevent such a problem, as most, if not all, library functions to access SQL databases allow you to do such a thing. This will, therefore, eliminate the need for complex expression recognition or escaping filtering functions.

Never, ever, expect your user to behave. Never expect him to comply with your instructions. Never expect him to always know what he's doing and always remember that for each user that doesn't quite know what he's doing, there's a user that knows too much. There are many ways the user

> Never assume the user will behave as expected.

input can mess with your program. Always check the values and use code statements to enforce the limits you describe in the documentation. Also, do not apply arbitrary limits to the length of the data your program should receive. If you need to apply limits, do it because those values make sense, not because you just feel like it. For instance, many command-line utilities of common UNIX systems have been developed with predetermined limits to the number of files a directory can have when they're called to act on that directory, while some other utilities deal quite gracefully with any number of files in a directory. If you develop your applications imposing such limitations, you may be sabotaging your own success. Examples of situations where such strict limitations should not be found are the number of files in a set or in a directory, the length of a path or file name, the length of the lines in a file and many other similar situations. Most of these limitations

> Do not impose arbitrary limits to the amount of data your program receives.

result from deciding during the project and implementation stage to use static data structures instead of dynamically allocated structures.

Another situation you need to be aware of is internationalization. Whenever you are using strings, or any type of data subject to localized settings, like a date or a number format, you need to take those aspects into account and be able to accept data in any valid format, regardless of the encoding, the date or number format. If you're developing a GUI[13] application, the graphical environment provides you with the tools (such as library calls and data in system structures) to allow you to detect the format of the input and deal with it. If you're developing a console application, you can inquire the console and the environment variables for the information you require.

4.7 Functions

As a first note, it's important to state that a lot, if not all, of what's described in these sections also applies to class methods, not only to functions. The complexity of writing functions and methods makes them vulnerable to some specific problems, some of which are described here.

---

13 *Graphical User Interface*

4.7.1 Error handling

Most functions have some sort of mechanism to report errors occurred during their execution. One common mechanism for error reporting is the return value of the function. However, there are many others, such as an external static variable (the "`errno`" variable in the standard C library, for example) and, if you are using an object oriented language with exception support, like C++ is, exceptions are also a good method. But it is up to the programmer to be careful and to always check for errors. It is important to never assume anything and to always have a way, if no other treatment is possible or desirable, to at least **provide a way to graciously deal with the error, even if it means to safely terminate the program.** You need not only to learn how to handle errors but, also, how to inform of their occurrence. To you, it will be a matter of context. However, if you're developing an API, you should come up with a way to report errors which is consistent across your whole API. It is important that, in error management, as in everything else, things are guided by intuitive rules that can be learned and automated.

> You can't predict the Universe, but you know anything can go wrong. Have a way to graciously terminate the program.

So, in C++, you have three basic ways to report errors: the return value, exceptions and a global static variable. The static variable, however, is far from being a safe way. There's the example of the "`errno`" variable, as referred above. Sometimes, in constrained situations, you may be forced to use such a construct, particularly if the conditions are well known, as in some embedded situations with extremely low resources. But, if you have the resources, then, don't compromise, apply appropriate methods. Use exceptions or return values. Having the static variable makes your code susceptible to problems when using threads and recursion. Also, you need to track your resources. You should never forget to check a value and never forget to release allocated memory when processing exceptions. It is easy to forget those situations and to assume the release happens just because an exception was triggered.

If you use exceptions, you can transport mostly any kind of information necessary to deal with the error. By providing you with a very powerful and flexible method to deal with error conditions, exceptions are an amazing feature of object oriented languages. Rather than using an explicit structure to verify error conditions, exceptions allow you to do so in a declarative manner. Using exceptions has some advantages over return values. Dealing with return values implies using conditional statements to verify those values. It is a realistic to think that conditional statements represent about a ten fold increase in the probability of introducing errors. This, of course, has the inconvenient side effect of reducing the quality of code and, therefore, increasing the development cost and the time to market. Other disadvantage of using the return values is that it introduces limitations to your functions when you want to actually return meaningful values from the processing made by your function. Often this is done by passing parameters by either pointer or reference, that your function manipulates. Furthermore, there's the problem of scalability. It is important to be able to easily introduce new condition checks and to allow other functions to process the error condition posterior to your processing, *ie.*, you may want to propagate the error condition, after dealing with it and, if you're using return values, you're forced to define explicit error propagation in your code:

```
1  int myfunc()
2  {
3    int l_error = hisfunc();
4
5    if(l_error) return(l_error);
6    else return(herfunc());
7  }
```

Notice that your code needs to examine the error and act based on it, before returning anything at all. It's a lot more proactive code you need to add. Meanwhile, exceptions are a much more elegant solution for most situations, for their declarative approach to this sort of situation. If you need to propagate errors, pass more information than a simple error code, and have a more structured approach to failure management, you can do so by using exceptions as they provide a fairly transparent way to deal with such situations. Be sure to check section 5.4 as it provides a more detailed explanation about exceptions.

4.7.2 Inline functions and methods

> Inline functions allow you to reduce dependency on the preprocessor, but use them carefully.

Inline functions allow the compiler to expand the code of those functions into the point of call. Using the "inline" keyword is not a guarantee that the compiler will actually expand the function. It's rather an indication, an hint to the compiler, letting it know that you think that function is a good candidate for inlining. You need to be careful with inlines. Depending on how you use them, they can make your code faster, smaller, slower or bigger. In some situations they reduce code size and increase speed, by removing unnecessary branches, which means that not only you're removing the jump and return instructions, but you're also preventing the CPU from flushing the cache, something it needs to do when any type of branch instruction occurs. They may also reduce code size and increase speed by allowing the compiler to reduce stack accesses and registers needed. But the opposite effect can also be verified in some situations. Incorrectly applied inlining can lead to increasing the code size, even if it improves performance in a localized analysis of the algorithm. And if the code grows enough, that particular speed improvement may be lost if the amount of available memory is small and the operating system is forced to swap out pages of the executable code more often.

Now, about the code macros. If you use code macros, you are also incurring in the same problem as with value macros mentioned in section 4.2.1.3, *ie.*, making it harder to debug. You are preventing the compiler from helping you with your coding, since the compiler will only see the already substituted code. In C you would use the preprocessor to create macros disguised as functions, to be used in places where reducing the function call overhead and/or making it somewhat type independent was desirable. However, there are new ways to achieve this in C++, using either inline functions or templates. One common example is the "`max()`" function, which returns the highest of two values. Take a look at this implementation:

```
#define max(a, b) (a > b ? a : b)
```

What's wrong with this picture? If someone (including you) is using your macro, and makes the mistake of using composed expressions instead of single symbols like a variable, a value, or a function call, you're in trouble. This happens because those expressions, when expanded, can do weird things with the precedence of the operators. And, then, you go and fix the macro, enclosing all the parameters in parenthesis, getting you to something like:

```
#define max(a, b) ((a > b) ? (a) : (b))
```

But you're not out of the woods, yet. As an exercise to the reader, try to figure out what's wrong with this macro. As a hint, try single operand operators and combinations that trigger different results on the macro. Now, going back to a real solution for this, there are two you can use. One implies that you write a different function for every type you wish to use, since it's based upon using simple inline functions. For instance, this is what you'd do for integers:

```
1  inline int max(int p_a, int p_b)
2  {
3      return(p_a > p_b ? p_a : p_b);
4  }
```

But, as you can see, you can use this function only with integers. You'd have to write a new function for each type you use. An easy solution for that problem would be the application of templates. Templates allow your code to be reused and they're really easy to apply to this example:

```
1  template <class T> inline const T&(const T & p_a,
2                                    const T & p_b
3                                    )
4  {
5    return(p_a > p_b ? p_a : p_b);
6  }
```

This will return a reference to "`p_a`" if "`p_a`" is bigger, and will return "`p_b`" if they are equal or "`p_b`" is bigger. You need to take this into account when using this methodology, as it may influence your program, when you're expecting references. Also, this template assumes, obviously, that the type of the parameters has an "`operator>()`" defined. Otherwise, it will generate a compilation error. All these examples make it obvious that you can decrease your dependency on the preprocessor. However, the preprocessor will still not become useless, but be careful about your choices.

4.7.3 Variable arguments

Historically, C has allowed some latitude when dealing with arguments. Usually, one would not need to previously declare a function and could use it directly. This, alone, was problematic, as the compiler had no way to verify the correctness of the arguments. C++ is a bit more brutal in regard to this, as it enforces the declaration of the functions before they can be used. This is good, because it helps to defend the programmer from himself. The declaration of a function prior to its use supplies the compiler with a larger amount of useful information to use when checking what the programmer is doing. When dealing with functions with variable arguments, however, things don't get any safer. By nature, both being relatively low-level languages, the way as variable arguments are handled doesn't allow for a very safe usage. It's completely in the programmer's hands to deal with this. One such function is declared as follows:

```
<return_type> funcname(<fixed_params> ...);
<fixed_params> = [<parameter_type parameter_name>, ]*
```

A very obvious example of a variable parameter function is "`printf`", as well as the remaining "`*printf`" family of functions:

```
int printf(const char *format, ...);
```

The function has only one fixed parameter, "`format`". This parameter is the only way the function has to know what has been passed to it. The parameter is a clue, given by the programmer, indicating what other parameters to expect beyond the format parameter and how to deal with them. The number of the parameters and their types are data that the code of the function isn't able to get from the compiler at any time, unless stated explicitly by the programmer. It is, then, easy to introduce a problem if the parameters passed and the format string do not match. Depending on the function, results may vary from simple aesthetic flaws to highly destructive crashes and data corruption.

To better understand what problems may arise from using variable arguments, it is important to understand how they are used and accessed. To write a function with variable arguments, you need to use the macros from the header "**stdarg.h**". In the past, right in the origins of C, no such macros were necessary. The fact that C was, at the time, limited to the original DEC PDP-11, made dealing with variable arguments a question of simple pointer arithmetic. However, the language evolved to actually be portable and a way to deal with other platforms transparently (without introducing dependencies on the business layer) was needed and, eventually, achieved. Because of that, today, there is "**stdarg.h**".

Three macros are needed to manage the parameters: "**va_start**", "**va_arg**" and "**va_end**". The "**va_start**" macro points to the last fixed argument of the function. It is mandatory that the function has, at least, one fixed argument, otherwise it will be impossible for the macros to locate the variable argument list. You should know that you are not supposed to use array or function types, register based parameters (among others) because, if you do, you'll be facing undefined behavior. This macro has the following prototype:

```
void va_start(va_list ap, param);
```

Before doing anything else, this is this macro that you need to call, since it will initialize the "**ap**" structure. The "**ap**" symbol, of "**va_list**" type, which you need to declare, has the objective to hold the data needed by the macros in order to provide you the variable arguments feature. This makes "**ap**" a variable you need to declare and track, since it has the information you need. The "**param**" parameter is the name of last fixed parameter of the function. That's how the macros track the variable parameters. An interesting fact about "**ap**", is that you can pass it to another function and have that function process the argument list. However, the caller function must not access "**ap**" as its value will be unknown and the only thing it can do with it is to pass it to "**va_end**", explained below. The "***printf**" family of functions uses this construct. Not all of them are directly variable argument functions. There are some, the "**v*printf**" functions that, instead of variable arguments, take a parameter of "**va_list**" type. The equivalent to the "**printf**" function, for example, "**vprintf**" has the following prototype:

```
int vprintf(const char * p_format, va_list p_ap);
```

This does come in handy, sometimes. You may find yourself writing a variable argument function that needs to have its arguments passed to one of the "**v*printf**" functions or even to some other function written by yourself.

Then, you have "**va_arg**". With this macro, you have access to the arguments. But you also need to be aware that only certain types can be used for arguments. This is the equivalent declaration of the macro:

```
param_type va_arg(va_list ap, param_type);
```

The "**ap**" structure will be changed with each call to "**va_arg**". Think of it as an iterator over the variable arguments list, which, in reality, it is. After extracting the arguments, you need to call "**va_end**" to perform clean up tasks:

```
void va_end(va_list ap);
```

Finally, you must never forget to use "**va_end**". Like many other things, in low level languages, undefined behavior is a plague. The best way to use variable arguments is to perform the entire processing at once, in a single run. If you need to revisit parameters, you'll have to begin the process again, starting with "**va_start**". To avoid this, the best thing you can do is to process the entire argument list once at the beginning of the function and store it in some way useful to your function that also allows random access.

4.7.4 Returning from a function

What you return from a function is just as important as what you pass to it. You call a function because you need it to do something for you, like performing some action or computing some value. As with parameters, you also need to be careful about what you make the function return. First, never try to return a local by reference or pointer. When the function exits, the object or variable will be destroyed. If it's a POD variable, you may be lucky to still be able to access the value, because even though the stack has already been popped, the memory hasn't been zeroed. However, it depends on your code whether that part of the memory has already been overwritten or not.

Also, don't return a value just because you can. If you need to return something, do it. If you don't, then don't complicate things.

4.7.5 Function overloading caveats

In C++ you have available the possibility of function and method overloading. This means that you can have several functions or methods with the same name, with different bodies, as long as the parameters make them distinguishable. Although this appears to be the same method, in fact, they are not, and the method used is determined at compile time. The compiler distinguishes between the several available methods by analyzing the types of the parameters. Overloaded functions and methods with the same name are supposed to perform similar or contextually equivalent tasks on different sets or types of parameters, when declared in the same context. But take the situation where you have defined the following functions:

```
void write(char * p_string);
void write(int p_number);
```

And then you attempt to do something like this:

```
write(NULL);
```

Just like that, your compiler got more confused than a bisexual teenager. This is what you'll get from, for example,

GCC[14]:

```
user@localhost:~/Tests$ g++ -c test.cpp
test.cpp: In function 'int main()':
test.cpp:9: error: call of overloaded 'write(NULL)' is
ambiguous
test.cpp:3: note: candidates are: void write(int)
test.cpp:4: note:                  void write(char*)
```

As you can see, GCC identified an ambiguity and informed of the available alternatives. The way to avoid this problem is to explicitly identify which of the functions to use by applying a cast:

```
write((int) NULL);
```

Suppose, now, that you have functions with the same name but a different number of parameters. If you are using default values for the parameters, you may end up experiencing the same problem, with different origins. Take the following trivial example, useful only for demonstration purposes:

```
void write(int p_param1);
void write(int p_param1, int p_param2 = 0);
```

And now you do:

```
write(0);
```

---

14 *GNU Compiler Collection*

You get exactly the same problem, but for different reasons:

```
test.cpp: In function 'int main()':
test.cpp:11: error: call of overloaded 'write(int)' is
ambiguous
test.cpp:3: note: candidates are: void write(int)
test.cpp:4: note:                 void write(int, int)
```

Therefore, you need to be careful. This time, you cannot "cast" your way out of the ambiguity. If, in your equivalent case, the "`write(int)`" and "`write(int, int = 0)`" functions are so different in what they do that you cannot remove the default value for the second parameter in the second function and retain exactly the same functionality, then you may need to reconsider. Be careful on how you design your API to avoid this kind of problems.

4.7.6 Notable functions

Some functions from the standard C library present some specificities that make them notable enough to justify a specific reference. Those functions are presented here.

4.7.6.1 The gets function

The purpose of the "`gets()`" function is to read a string of characters from the keyboard and store it in a buffer it receives as a parameter. If, with a recent compiler, you attempt to use this function, you will, most likely, be presented with a warning telling you that such function is dangerous. The explanation is in the function's prototype, if you pay attention to it:

```
char * gets(char * p_buffer);
```

The string of characters that "`gets()`" accepts ends when it finds a newline or when it reaches the end of the keyboard queue. Since the user is supposed to allocate and pass the buffer to the function and there is no way to tell the function how big the buffer is, "`gets()`" simply writes characters to the buffer until there are no more characters to write, regardless of the buffer size. This means that, if there are more characters in the keyboard queue than the buffer can receive, a common error called buffer overflow will occur, the consequences of which may vary and include segmentation faults that kill your program, security flaws that can be exploitable by mischievous third parties and overwriting data from contiguous buffers. You should consider the usage of "`gets()`" as a developer's sin and use "`fgets()`" instead and remember that like this one, many other functions may present the same problems.

4.7.6.2 The *printf family of functions

As mentioned before, this family of functions is interesting because an enlarged set of problems can be introduced if such functions aren't used correctly. Most of the problems arise from the fact that these functions allow for an arbitrary number of parameters. Recall the prototype for the "`printf()`" function:

```
int printf(const char * format, ...);
```

You need to be careful about these functions because they

are somewhat sensitive. It is common to make mistakes such as incompatible types of the parameters or incorrect number of parameters. For instance, you may use "`%s`" to tell "`printf()`" you want to print a string but, because of some mistake, the parameter in the corresponding slot in the parameter list is an integer instead of a pointer to a character string. If, for some cosmic joke, the value in the integer, is equal to the pointer of the string, the program ends up doing what it is supposed to. Or maybe not. One thing you should never hope for is that a program presents the correct result despite the fact that it is improperly implemented. **Do not allow yourself to do "band-aid based" programming. Your program should be properly coded from the start, and not be a collection of eleventh-hour solutions that are barely held together by duct tape.**

> Don't do "band-aid" based coding. If you're doing something, do it right from the start, not as a collection of duct tape fixes.

4.8 Managing temporary storage

"There is more than one way to skin a cat". This expression comes to make a bit more sense if you gain enough experience with the history of the UNIX API. Should you someday need to create temporary files, you'll be faced with a few distinct ways to do so. One of the ways is based upon asking the system to generate a unique name for a file, in a path of your choosing, and you'll be left with the task of creating and opening the file. While at first glance this seems trivial, you need to remember that modern operating systems allow several threads to run in parallel. Whatever the number of cores of the computer, there will be several processes competing for the resources in the computer. Between the time when your process received a unique name for your temporary file and the time it managed to actually create it, the process might have been preempted and other processes may have done horrible things in that interval.

There are three well known functions to create the name for the temporary file: "**mktemp**", "**tempnam**" and "**tmpnam**". The differences between them are mostly cosmetic, differing only in the algorithm used to generate the distinct filename and whether they allow to specify a prefix pathname. The code that follows should provide you with a reasonable example on how you would create a temporary file using this method. Please consult the appropriate manuals for any reference to the functions.

```
char * l_tempname = tempnam("/tmp/", "tmpfile");

FILE * l_file = fopen(l_tempname, "w+");

// do your stuff here

fclose(l_file);

free(l_tempname);
```

If your process happens to be preempted right between lines 1 and 3, then another process may have found a way to predict or even to discover the name your process got for your temporary file. Such a process might have had the time to, before your process gets another time slice, create that file itself, with permissions which allow your process to read and write from it, but whose owner is not the user under which your process runs, but the user that owns the malignant process. This means that such malignant process will have full access to the data your process dumps into that temporary file. And, of course, there is one thing you cannot forget to do after you're finished with your temporary file: delete it.

There are, however, appropriate ways to, today, open temporary files without incurring in this danger. There are functions that, atomically, not only produce a name, but also an open file for your process to use immediately, because they cannot be preempted and, therefore, are not susceptible to such attacks. There are two functions you can use, "**tmpfile**" and "**mkstemp**". The first function creates and opens an empty binary file which is automatically disposed of as soon as the file pointer is closed. This is an example on how to do so:

```
1  FILE * l_file = tmpfile();
2  // remember to check the pointer for error codes, ok?
3  ...
4  // do your stuff
5  ...
6  fclose(l_file);
```

This function has its own limitations, however. For once, you have no access to the name of the created file. Also, the permissions with which the file is created are undetermined. Then you have the second function, "**mkstemp**". It's an improvement on both "**tmpfile**" and "**mktemp**". Not only does the same atomic job of creating and opening the file, but also allows you to select a prefix pattern for the file. More than that, it creates the file with the "**O_EXCL**" flag, which ensures that not only the file doesn't exist at that time, but also that no one else touches it. And it is created with permissions "**0600**", guaranteeing that only the user running the process that created the file can access it. This function returns a regular open file descriptor and stores the file name in the buffer you pass to it. Unlike "**tmpfile**", you're supposed to write your code in such a way that it deletes the file when you're finished.

```
const char l_template[] = "/tmp/tmp.XXXXXX";

// PATH_MAX is from limits.h
char l_name[PATH_MAX];

// copying the template
// shouldn't overwrite string constants
strcpy(l_name, l_template);

int l_file = mkstemp(l_name);
...
// do your stuff
...
close(l_file);
unlink(l_name);
```

You may have noticed the usage of "**PATH_MAX**". That symbol is defined in the C header "**limits.h**" and it is, theoretically, the maximum size of a pathname. Theoretically, because the reality is a bit different. The value of that symbol is different in all operating systems. Truth be told, not only the value is different, but the way the system calls and libraries react to it in each operating system is different too. For instance, the call "**getcwd()**" (get current working directory) fails if the size of the path is longer than "**PATH_MAX**" on Linux but, on OS X, as long as the buffer passed to it is long enough, there is no problem. There are some calls that rely on "`PATH_MAX`" too much and do not allow you to inform them of the size of your buffer.

On UNIX systems, you should also pay attention to the "`TMPDIR`" environment variable and, on Windows, to the "`TEMP`", environment variable. Those variables contain the path for the system's temporary files directory. While it's in your hands to decide where to store your temporary files, it may be advisable to use those folders.

As an additional note, it may be interesting to explore additional features: some operating systems (and some specific filesystems) allow you to activate specific file attributes that mark it as a special case for deletion, enforcing the operating system to zero fill all the sectors that belonged to the file whenever they are released. This will help make sure that the contents of the file can't be examined by doing a low-level examination of the disk sectors where the file was stored.

5 Classes and objects

This subject is extensive enough to justify a separate chapter. Object-oriented programming is the foundation of a lot of modern programming languages. It is an efficient and ingenious way to ease development, produce safer and higher quality code, and to better reflect the real world in a computationally useful mathematical model.

5.1 Your API

The first thing you need to make sure you get right is your API. Having a well defined API is one of the most important steps in writing a good piece of software. You need to have it well organized, well defined, free of ambiguities and as intuitive and self documented as possible.

5.1.1 Good Ideas

5.1.1.1 Organize your global namespace

If you don't subdivide your global namespace, it gets bloated really fast. Organizing your global scope, applying context to elements is important, so that you have something elegant and functional. Use different namespaces for different contexts. If necessary, chain namespaces.

5.1.1.2 Proper interfaces

Be sure to let interfaces define your API. Your interfaces should be minimal and complete. What does this mean? It means that they have as few members as possible, without duplicating functionality, while still providing every reasonable function the user of your API might expect from it. This is important to make sure your API is simple and concise, while being fully featured. For more information, check section 5.3.2.4.

5.2 Constructors and destructors

Constructors are the methods that initialize your objects.

They are automatically called when the object is created and they prepare the object for being used. Destructors are just the opposite. They finalize the object and allow the release of its resources. Because of that, there are certain rules one has to follow and certain problems that are not immediately apparent.

While dealing with objects, you need to take into account some details. One of these is that local objects are created in the reverse order of their construction. The same happens with arrays of objects.

5.2.1 Bad ideas

5.2.1.1 Chaining constructors

One common mistake unexperienced programmers do, is to try constructor chaining. In classes with more than one constructor, it could make sense to avoid duplicating code. However, calling another constructor is not the way to do it, in C++. Trying to call a constructor will result in initializing a new local object within the current object constructor. It will not call the constructor of the current object. Usually there are two ways to solve this. If possible, try to use default values for the parameters of the constructor so you can combine constructors. If not, your remaining alternative is to create a separate method that you can call whatever you like, typically private, into which you would move all the code intended to be shared among constructors and then call that method from the constructors.

5.2.1.2 Using exceptions in destructors

Well, yes, it is actually a really bad idea to use exceptions inside destructors. This is because exceptions should not be thrown during a stage called "stack unwinding". This is the stage between the moment an exception is thrown and the moment it is caught. During this stage, all the objects in the stack are destroyed since the stack frames are eliminated. What then? The C++ runtime code, that invisible code that the compiler adds when it compiles your code, is left without knowing which exception handler to jump to. The best way to deal with this is to avoid throwing exceptions from destructors, so you can reduce the possibility of messing with the stack unwinding process.

5.2.1.3 Explicitly calling a destructor on a local

When the object reaches the end of its life inside a block, you can be sure its destructor is always called. You should not attempt to dispose of the object by explicitly calling its destructor, because it will be called again later on. If you need the object to close itself before the end of the block, you should move the necessary code into another method, making it safe to call. That same method could be called by the destructor if necessary. You should also not try to call the destructor on objects created by "`new`". It may work, or not, in closing the object, but you will not get the object's memory released. There's a reason for "`delete`" to exist. The only time you should explicitly call the destructor is on objects created by "placement new".

5.2.1.4 Calling virtual functions

Within the constructor, you should not attempt to call a virtual function hoping it will call the function from the derived class. That, simply put, doesn't work. Calling virtual functions is only available after the object has been fully constructed. Because the object is constructed following derivation order, if your constructor was able to call the overriding function, there would be the possibility of that function trying to access members yet uninitialized. Because of that problem, the language imposes that limitation. If you try to call any virtuals, you'll end up calling the function on the same class of the constructor you're calling it from. This is a simple example, and although there would be no need, in this particular example, to actually call the method from the constructors, it's there just to illustrate the explanation:

```
1   class CPlayer
2   {
3     protected:
4       int m_life;
5
6     public:
7       virtual void resetHealth() { m_life = 100; };
8
9       CPlayer(): m_points(0)
10      {
11        resetHealth();
12      }
13  };
14
15  class CHumanPlayer: public CPlayer
16  {
17    protected:
18      int m_shield;
19
20    public:
21      virtual void resetHealth()
22      {
23        CPlayer::resetHealth();
```

```
24
25          m_shield = 100;
26      }
27
28      CHumanPlayer(): m_shield(100) {}
29  };
```

If you were hoping that, when an object of type "**CHumanPlayer**" was created, line 11 would call "**CHumanPlayer::resetHealth()**", I'm sorry to disappoint you.

There are ways to go around this without compromising the safety of your program, but complicating the code a bit. One way is to create a secondary constructor method, from which you perform the remainder of the construction steps. But, then, you'll face a problem. Making the construction of an object a two-step process will bring up the probability of making mistakes if you're not following the steps right. To prevent this, you either automate yourself, and everyone else that uses your class, not to fail, or you choose a different path. This different path might be a better alternative, creating a factory method to return an object, that not only creates it, but also calls the second stage constructor method. To avoid problems, you may want to prevent anyone from creating the object any other way than by calling the factory method. You should be familiar with this pattern and recognize that the smart thing to do is to make the constructor private or protected, as seen on the following example:

```
1   class CExampleClass
2   {
```

```
3      protected:
4        CExampleClass();
5        void init();
6
7      public:
8        static CExampleClass & createObject()
9        {
10         CExampleClass * l_object;
11         l_object->init();
12         return(* l_object);
13       }
14   };
```

5.2.1.5 Relying in the order of static initialization

When you have static objects in your project, be careful about dependencies between them. If one object is dependent on the other, but if the dependent object is initialized before its dependency, then you have a problem. If they're declared on the same file, it is up to you to make sure you have them declared in the proper order. It gets worse if the variables are declared on separate files. Remember that for variables to be accessible from different compilation units, they must be marked as externals. Trivial example follows:

CGame.h

```
1   class CGame
2   {
3     CGame();
4   };
5
6   #ifndef __CGAME_CPP__
7   extern CGame G_gameboard;
8   #endif
```

Edition Zero - Classes and objects

CPlayer.h

```
1  #include "CGame.h"
2
3  class CPlayer
4  {
5     protected:
6        CGame & m_myboard;
7
8     public:
9        CPlayer();
10 };
```

CGame.cpp

```
1  #define __CGAME_CPP__
2
3  #include "CGame.h"
4
5  CGame G_gameboard;
6
7  // ... everything else
```

CPlayer.cpp

```
1  #include "CPlayer.h"
2
3  CPlayer::CPlayer(): m_myboard(G_gameboard)
4  {
5     // ... stuff
6  }
```

In that case, they are going to be initialized in any order the linker decides to link them together and, as you can imagine, that can cause a myriad of problems. Be careful about doing such a thing. There are several approaches you can use to deal with this situation. An obvious one is to dynamically construct the objects when they are first needed. This way, you can ensure that, when they are needed, they're ready. One way to achieve this is to use local static variables inside global functions that return the object by reference. That, with a little preprocessor magic, can masquerade the function call. However, even this approach has its downsides. There are two variants of this approach. The first is to use a local static object directly.

```
1  CGame & G_gameboard()
2  {
3    static l_gameboard;
4
5    return(l_gameboard);
6  }
```

But, if any of the destructors of the objects dependent on this one need to access it and the object gets destroyed before its dependencies, or if the object's address is passed to any other static object, there's really no way to know for sure what would happen, but functioning well is unlikely to be the best case scenario. If the constructors of the dependent objects use the pivot object, then the compiler will likely guarantee that the objects are destroyed in the right order. Then you have the second approach, which would be to have not the object itself, but a pointer to the object.

```
1  CGame & G_gameboard()
2  {
3    static * l_gameboard = new CGame();
4
5    return(* l_gameboard);
6  }
```

However, there's still the problem that even though there will actually be no memory leak because the memory of the whole process will be released when it ends, since the object will be effectively lost, its constructor will not be called, so any cleanup actions you might want it to perform when it ends, won't take place. There are, of course, ways to go around this, but you're already using one workaround. Are you sure you want to use workaround on workaround?

5.2.1.6 Unnecessary default constructors

If you don't need a default constructor, avoid creating one. A default constructor needs no external information to create the object. There are many situations where default constructors are important but, in many other situations, there's no real way to create an object without external information, since there are rarely any relevant default values.

5.2.2 Good ideas

5.2.2.1 Using initialization lists

It is a better idea to use initialization lists rather than explicitly assigning the values to the members in the body of the constructor. The usage of initialization lists allows the compiler to optimize the constructor. Furthermore, you cannot initialize constant members by assignment, only in initialization lists. Additionally, to take full advantage of using them, the order of the initialization must be the same order in which the members were declared. Otherwise, in the best case scenario, your compiler will issue a message warning you of the problem. Of course, there are situations where using initialization lists may not be the best choice. One such example is when you have two constructors, one of which has to initialize the members in a different order from the other one due to dependencies. One of the constructors might actually do fine with initialization lists, but the other will not be. In that case, you're left with explicitly assigning the value to the member.

5.2.2.2 Using "this" inside the constructor

You can safely use the "`this`" pointer inside a constructor to refer to the members of that constructor's class. Because of the reasons explained in section 5.2.1.4, you will not be able to access methods from derived classes overriding virtuals from the constructor's class. When the constructor starts executing, all the data members of that class are guaranteed to have already been constructed. Hence, you can safely access them. But be careful when passing the "`this`" pointer to a function external to the class, a method of another class, or even a constructor of another class.

5.2.2.3 Using exceptions in constructors

If anything fails during the constructor execution, you need to warn the caller. Since constructors provide no means to return a value, you have only one choice: exceptions. And, as described in section 4.7.1 and will see again in section 5.4, they're usually the best choice. You catch the exception and deal with it. However, you must remember that if the exception is thrown inside the constructor, there will be no calling of the destructor. One way to deal with that problem is to have a data member record all the things that need to be undone.

There is also an alternative to using exceptions in situations where using them is either undesirable or not possible. In those cases, you can probably live with having a data member (as well as the appropriate getter function) to hold an error code. This means that you will have to delete the object, have it record how far the constructor managed to set up the object so it can rollback the changes in the destructor, and you will have to go back to the old story of creating conditional control structures with "`if`"/ "`else`" or "`switch`"/ "`case`".

5.2.2.4 Dynamic memory? Copy constructor.

If your class has dynamically allocated memory, you may need to consider writing your own copy constructor, which, of course, depends on the structure of your class. If you don't, the compiler will generate a copy-constructor for you but the member pointers will be pointing to the same blocks of memory. You really may not want that. Therefore, you need to be careful and make sure your copy-constructor takes that into account. For the same reason you may want to write your own overload of the assignment operator.

5.3 Inheritance specifics

Although a common belief, and actually a possibility, the reason why inheritance exists is not for code reuse but, primarily, to allow a design by contract model, by introducing a method to obtain compliance with a predefined interface. To be able to do proper object oriented coding, you need to really strengthen your grasp of the concept of inheritance. You should also get a basic idea of what the compiler does when you call a virtual method. Therefore, this section presents you with a simplified explanation to what goes on when that happens, hoping this will help you better deal with your code. Features like Run-Time Type Information and Virtual Inheritance can make it much harder to explain, and are going to be left out for now.

When you call a virtual method, the runtime system refers to the "v-table", a table placed in static memory, containing the list and the pointers to the methods of the class, through which the calls are going to be translated. Each virtual method "owns" a slot in the "v-table". Only one instance of the "v-table" exists in a process, it is a static piece of data. Your objects have an hidden pointer called the "v-pointer". This pointer points to that object's class "v-table". There is only one "v-pointer" per object, regardless of the number of ancestors in the inheritance chain, but there are as many "v-tables" as classes defined. When the method is called, the runtime checks the "v-table" slot corresponding to that method and transfers control to the method, passing to it, as the first parameter, the pointer to the object and the parameters you supplied as the remaining parameters. Translated into assembly code, this does not get much more complicated than half a dozen instructions, maybe less. If you understood what's been explained, by now you should have realized that calling a virtual method is still almost as fast as calling a non virtual method or a function, that the number of ancestors in the inheritance chain do not influence the performance and that the size of an object of a class with virtual methods gets only negligible overhead compared to classes with no virtual methods, since they grow, usually, only by a pointer size.

5.3.1 Bad ideas

5.3.1.1 Changing member visibility

With public inheritance, trying to change the visibility of an inherited method is a really bad idea. The method had a certain visibility in the parent class for a reason. If you try to hide a method that was public, you are subverting the semantics of the whole thing with undesirable consequences in the understanding of the code.

5.3.1.2 Being too literal with notions in classes

While object oriented programming allows you to layout a reflection of the real world into a program, it is sometimes hard to do it correctly or to decide for a specific path. There may be many ways a situation can be mapped into a set of classes and relations. Sometimes, the best way to do it may not be the most realistic, just because explaining things to a computer is much different from explaining them to a person. If you rely too much on a strict interpretation of reality, or if you make the mistake of being too literal while designing your classes, you may end up making your life harder and losing the benefits of using object-oriented programming. Be careful. You've been warned.

5.3.2 Good ideas

5.3.2.1 Virtual constructors

Suppose you have the following situation. You want to be able to clone an object, regardless of the type. You have the pointer to the object, but you don't know if that object is really of that type, or of a derived type. You can't, therefore, just use the regular copy constructor. How to solve this? You create a virtual method. The name is up to you but it's common practice to use the name "`clone()`", for this particular situation. Then you make each derived class implement that method. This way you can always get a copy of the object, appropriately built. Inside the "`clone()`" method, you can actually use the copy constructor, because you'll be inside the actual class of the object you want to clone. With little variation, you can also create a companion method called "`create()`" which, instead of cloning the object, creates a new object of the same type.

5.3.2.2 Virtual destructors

You won't always need to make your destructors virtual, but there are times when they absolutely must be virtual. If you are faced with a situation where an object may be destroyed by deleting a pointer of an ancestor class of that object, then you should make your destructor virtual. If you have any virtual methods, then your destructor must be virtual. Making your destructor virtual brings no further cost to the objects of your class if it has virtual functions, because the objects will already have the "v-pointer". And you need your destructor to be virtual because if it's not, the destructor called is the one of the type of the pointer. That would leave the object only partially destroyed and, for sure, you want it completely and properly destroyed. You should also remember that if the destructor of the base class has already been marked as virtual, the destructors of all derived classes will be virtual as well.

5.3.2.3 Protecting derived classes from breaking

There will be some classes that you will want to design in such a manner that helps preventing derived classes from suffering the results of changes in the internals. One thing you should always do is to document those changes. And another thing you could do is to make those elements private, offering protected methods to access them. Make sure such a method is an inline method, so it does not incur in any performance and code size penalties, should the compiler be unable to figure out for itself to inline it.

5.3.2.4 Using abstract classes and interfaces

Interfaces are the most important part of your project. They allow you to define a clear architecture, they're the hardest part to define and they're what actually allows a "by-contract" design. Implementing the classes is a piece of cake when compared to designing a proper set of interfaces. C++ doesn't have a specific set of keywords for interfaces, but it does allow you to write abstract classes. By using purely abstract base classes, you are able to create interfaces for your classes that represent the abstract concept you want to expose and manipulate. To create a purely abstract class, all the methods in that class must be purely virtual. From there you can move into deriving that interface to implement it and actually make your program run.

5.3.2.5 Having private virtuals

There are many situations where this is actually a good idea (exceptions apply, as with everything else). You should not make all your members private, only those you want to protect from being called by members of other classes but that you still need them to be replaceable by implementations of derived classes. This is common when you have non-virtuals of base classes that need to call internal virtuals.

5.4 Exceptions

Exceptions are a very flexible mechanism for handling abnormal conditions in the program flow. They provide you with a powerful way to both report and discover run-time errors. They are a much safer approach to handling those errors than any other method, such as return values and static variables. They are scalable, easily readable and allow you to specify error treatment conditions in a declarative manner instead of having to explicitly write conditional code to decode the error. They are a good idea for having a structured and consistent way to do error reporting when you are building an API.

If you want a truly structured approach to exception handling, one thing you must do is to **define a base exception class from which all**

> Use a base exception class for all your exceptions, make it inherit from STL's std:exception

your exceptions derive. This allows you to have a wildcard solution for situations where you do not wish to deal with each type of exception separately. Furthermore, if you make that base type exception derive from the Standard Template Library's "`std::exception`" or any of STLs exceptions, you can take advantage of the facilities that STL classes already have and increase compatibility with the STL. While it is true that, in C++, you can use anything as an exception, it doesn't mean you should. Using an instantiation of a class provides you with an appropriate framework for producing important and detailed run-time error information, something which, depending on the situation, is much harder, if not impossible, to do if you use any type of POD data. You have simple ways to do things efficiently, so use them.

You may need to gather more important about the conditions that originated an error. Doing it directly in the exception object, while in debug mode, allows you to do so and, with some effort, you can come up with the means to generate a rudimentary artificial exception stack trace. A stack trace is a listing that reports the function call path taken by a process when it generates an exception. There are libraries especially designed to do this at a lower level, directly accessing the stack frame of the process. However, the success of such libraries heavily depends on the optimization switches and the compiler used. If, for any reason, a specific compiler option known as "omitting the frame pointer" is applied, such method is impossible. The approach suggested, however, could have that in mind and be higher level, being, therefore, more resilient to compiler options and compiler choices, and able to be used even if necessary to do so in release mode. If you are wondering why it would be necessary to do so in release mode, don't. The explanation is simple. You may want to enable your product to produce error reports that can automatically be sent to you, like many systems in the market do. It is not advisable, however, against enabling the option to "omit the frame pointer". This is an option that is usually enabled to increase performance. However, the performance gain is known to be fairly reduced, around 5%, and you lose a fairly important means of diagnostic. In the end, hardly any compiler optimization is able to beat a properly written algorithm.

Now, having an idea on how to produce the error signals, you have to be able to catch them. The language allows you to catch them in three different ways: by value, by pointer and by reference. The mechanism is the same as with functions. However, doing so by value, when using class based exceptions, is not very efficient, as it implies that a copy of the exception object is made. If you have error propagation, then you'll have several copies of the object. It is inefficient in speed and space. It is only recommend if you're using a POD type as the exception (and using POD types is not recommended). Catching by pointer provides you with a way to avoid copies and you can pass complex structures. However, when an exception is caught by pointer, the final catcher in an error propagation chain will be responsible for deleting the exception. Not doing so introduces a memory leak. Also, the code that generates the exception must throw the pointer to the object, not the object. And, finally, you have the option of catching by reference. If you catch by reference, you do not have to worry about deleting the exception. You have all the functionality, you can propagate

> Prefer catching exceptions by reference.

error conditions and you reduce the possibility of memory leaks.

5.5 Friends

The "`friend`" keyword brings you a whole new set of possibilities. They allow a class to grant another class or function access to its internals. The idea behind this concept is not to break encapsulation or give you a way to go around it. It is actually to improve encapsulation by giving you a mechanism to strengthen the connection between tightly integrated elements. It's not something you should avoid, it's something you need to use with care and discretion. It can be, semantically and depending on the way it's applied, an equivalent to providing a public method to access internal data. You must never forget that "friendship", isn't both ways. It must be explicitly declared to achieve that effect. Also, it cannot be inherited. A class A may have access to a class B, but descendants of class A do not inherit the access to B. And there is no transitivity of "friendship". If you have a class A friend of class B, which in turn is friend of class C, it doesn't mean A is friend of C.

5.6 Operator overloading

Being able to overload operators allows you to have a straightforward and visually intuitive way for writing code. But it also gives templates their versatility, allowing you to implement the code with a syntax that can approach the semantics of the problem you're trying to solve. They can complicate the development of a class to which the overloaded operators apply, but they improve productivity for the users of those class.

5.6.1 Good ideas

5.6.1.1 *Keeping the semantics*

Although you can make your operators do just about everything, in the name of good development practices, try to keep the meaning of the operators at least similar or related to their original meanings. That will help keep the code readable, organized and self documented. That, in turn, will reduce the time needed by users of your API to learn it, as well as the amount of flaws introduced. Also, don't start overloading everything just because you can. Do it if, when, and because you need to.

When overloading arithmetic operators, it is a good idea to try and make it so that you get equivalent results to those expected in arithmetic operations. For example, suppose your class defines "`operator+()`" and "`operator-()`". It would be a good idea to have "`(lhs + rhs - rhs) == lhs`". Also, for those kind of operators, that return a new value without tainting the operands, when you're overloading them for classes, there are a few special considerations to take into account. First, you should return the result by value. If you return by reference, you'll have trouble deciding who would own the object and how to deal with disposing of it. You should also follow the behavior of not changing any of the source operands. You should only cause any changes to the operands if those operators cause changes to their operands when applied to the POD types. In summary, you should maintain the operator consistency across all types.

Additionally, you need to remember that, while you can overload most operators in C++, you cannot alter the precedence or associativity. These are fixed characteristics of each operator and, when designing your code, you must be aware of them.

5.6.1.2 Protecting your assignment operators

When you're dealing with the assignment operator, you need to be particularly careful. If you are overloading it, you must write your code to check for the possibility of an object being assigned to itself. Although it is unlikely that someone will be doing something like "x = x;", it is possible that, due to reference and pointer traveling, somewhere, along the code, such situation arises. And strange and tortuous things happen. Since the assignment operator should deal with references, there are ways you can prevent this situation. Sometimes you will not need to explicitly handle self assignment, if your class is simple enough for the handling of its members to be self protecting. But if you do need an explicit method to handle self assignment, then one solution, is to check the pointers of both members of the comparison to verify whether they are, or not, the same object:

```
1   CPlayer & CPlayer::operator=(CPlayer const & l_rhs)
2   {
3       if(this != &l_rhs)
4       {
5           // do your stuff here
6       }
7       return(* this);
```

```
8    }
```

Another solution is to create a temporary copy using the copy constructor of the object, and then perform the assignment based on that temporary object.

There's one other thing you need to take into account when dealing with assignment operators. If you're overloading the operator, you need to call the assignment operator of the base class. Should you not create the assignment operator for your derived class, the compiler will create an assignment operator for you that calls the base class assignment operator. Also, be sure to return a reference to "`*this`". Doing so allows you to daisy chain assignments and correctly take advantage of its associativity.

5.6.1.3 Using prefix operators

It is generally better to use prefix operators rather than postfix ones. This means that you might be better off using "`++ x;`" than "`x ++;`". The reason for this is that a prefix operator is usually faster, and never slower, than the postfix version. It doesn't make a difference for POD types. However, for objects it does make a huge difference, since the postfix operator may create a copy of the object. You need to be aware that they are different and, if you're using them in an expression, you need to take that into account since it may alter the results. But, when you are using the operator as an isolated statement, the best solution may be to use the prefix version.

5.6.1.4 Dynamic memory? Assignment overload

For the reasons explained in section 5.2.2.4, you may want to create your own assignment operator. Refer to that section for more information.

5.7 Binary trees safety

Binary trees are one of the most important data storage algorithms. These data structures are relatively balanced in terms of efficiency versus performance and access performance versus alteration performance. There are a lot of implementations and variations from the basic binary tree, but even the simplest implementation can be screwed up if proper attention isn't paid to the code. This section's objective is not to teach you what binary trees are or how to write a complete implementation of them, but about some typical problems you might find when implementing them yourself.

One example of an implementation and usage situation is the "`std::map`". This class provides, in C++, the equivalent functionality to an associative array, also known as a dictionary. The simplest array relates a numerical sequential index to an element. An associative array, on the other hand, is a special type of array that relates keys of any type, frequently strings, to the values. The C++ language does not provide such functionality directly in the language, therefore the only possible way to use it, is through specially implemented classes, in this case, the "`std::map`" from the Standard Template Library. Self-balancing binary search trees, because of their characteristics, are excellent for dictionaries. They allow for almost limitless insertion of elements and very fast searches, since access time is proportional to log(n), having O(log(n)) complexity.

The simplest element in a binary tree is the node. Binary trees are composed of nodes, each of them able to have at most two child nodes. A node with no children is called a leaf, a node with children is called a subtree, and the top node in the tree, the one with no parents, is called the root. Nodes are moved around, inserted, deleted and searched for. Should you implement your own binary tree and node classes, there are certain details you need to be careful about, which are common rookie mistakes. Take the following code as an example node class:

```
1   class CNode
2   {
3     protected:
4       CNode * m_left,
5             * m_parent,
6             * m_right;
7
8     public:
9       CNode();
10      CNode * set_left(CNode * p_node);
11      CNode * set_right(CNode * p_node);
12      ~CNode();
13  };
```

For this first analysis, forget about the data in the node. It'll be dealt with later. But, for now, take a look at this implementation. You may have noticed the choice of having the "**set_left()**" and "**set_right()**" methods return a pointer to another "**CNode**". The logic behind this is simple and useful. If you are replacing an already existing child, you have two choices. The first choice is to delete that child and recursively delete all its descendants. The second choice is to keep the old subtree and return it so it can be dealt with later. In this specific example, it's been chosen to keep the old subtree. This allows for some extra consistency checks and data retrieving, but it implies that the calling function is responsible for deleting the subtree.

Now imagine what the "set_left()" method does. There's no need to go deep into "set_right()", since it does exactly the same thing as "set_left()", symmetrically. Your first instinct will, perhaps, tell you to implement the method like this:

```
1  CNode * CNode::set_left(CNode * p_node)
2  {
3    CNode * l_oldnode = this->m_left;
4
5    this->m_left = p_node;
6
7    return(l_oldnode);
8  }
```

This seems apparently good code. You save the old child node (line 3), you replace it by the new child node in the "p_node" parameter (line 5), and then you return the old child node node (line 7). What's wrong with this picture? Remember that you are returning the old child node... and you haven't touched it yet. That node still "thinks" that the current node is its parent node. If you are deleting a node, you want it to delete its descendants, but you also want it to tell his parent that he is gone. That is done by setting the pointer in the parent to null.

So, this could be our destructor:

```
CNode::~CNode()
{
  if(this == this->m_parent->m_left)
    this->m_parent->m_left = NULL;
  else this->m_parent->m_right = NULL;

  delete(m_left);
  delete(m_right);
}
```

Apparently, there are no problems with this implementation. But that couldn't be farther from the truth. This is often the first implementation unexperienced developers write. One of the things you were told before was to never assume anything, and this code is as presumptuous as it could be. Should you attempt to delete a parent-less node returned by the "**set_left()**", this code will blow up in your face. The destructor will first attempt to verify if it is the left child of its parent. Since it will find out it is not, because it has been replaced, it will assume it was the right child. It will, then, overwrite the pointer to the right child with "**NULL**", which will immediately result in a whole subtree being lost and turned into a memory leak, as it will be inaccessible.

The destructor can be improved by enforcing a check for the right child pointer as well:

```
CNode::~CNode()
{
  if(this == this->m_parent->m_left)
    this->m_parent->m_left = NULL;
```

```
5       else if(this == this->m_parent->m_right)
6         this->m_parent->m_right = NULL;
7
8       delete(m_left);
9       delete(m_right);
10   }
```

However, although this now works better and prevents you from overwriting any of the nodes wrongfully, it's yet far from perfect. This destructor implementation still assumes the node has a valid pointer to the parent. However, even if "**m_parent**" pointer isn't "**NULL**", it may still be an invalid pointer, should the parent have already been deleted. This implies that the implementation of "**set_left()**" is incorrect or, at best, incomplete. This would be a more acceptable implementation:

```
1    CNode * CNode::set_left(CNode * p_node)
2    {
3      CNode * l_oldnode = this->m_left;
4
5      if(NULL != l_oldnode) l_oldnode->m_parent = NULL;
6
7      this->m_left = p_node;
8      this->m_left->m_parent = this;
9
10     return(l_oldnode);
11   }
```

By setting the parent pointer to "**NULL**" immediately in the "**set_left()**" method (and remember, all of this also applies to the "**set_right()**" method), you are making sure that the old child "knows" it has been turned into an orphan. And you also have to verify that the child you're removing actually exists and that the branch is not empty (line 5). After that, you only need to make sure the new child knows who's its daddy (line 8). Revisiting the destructor, now with the appropriate corrections:

```
1   CNode::~CNode()
2   {
3      delete(m_left);
4      delete(m_right);
5
6      if(NULL != this->m_parent)
7      {
8         if(this == this->m_parent->m_left)
9            this->m_parent->m_left = NULL;
10        else if(this == this->m_parent->m_right)
11           this->m_parent->m_right = NULL;
12     }
13
14  }
```

Now the node knows if it is an orphan, or not. And the checking for the right node is kept, should any other problem in the code, possibly not of your doing, break consistency. Remember that it is safe to use "**delete**" directly to remove the children, even if there are none, because, if there are none, the values will be "**NULL**" and "**delete**" safely ignores "**NULL**" pointers. All these aspects mentioned are situations you need to be careful about, be it in a binary tree or in any other algorithm. Dangling pointers, memory leaks, overwritten data, are problems you will face in a daily basis. As an exercise to the reader, try to figure out how to correct the "**set_left()**" and "**set_right()**" methods in order for them to be able to receive a "**NULL**" as the parameter (to simply remove a node from the tree) or to receive a node that already belongs to another tree (simply put, to move a node from a tree to another). About moving nodes from parent to parent, be careful. You may need to check for circular links, as something wrong with the code may end up making a node a child of one of its direct or indirect descendants.

6 Optimizations

Now that you've had some pointers on almost everything else, here are some tips on optimizing your program to reduce its memory consumption and footprint, and to increase performance. Also, you'll be told about some optimizations the compiler is able to do by itself, so that you are able to understand what the compiler will do with your code. It is a sad fact that nowadays most programmers have been poorly trained and have been taught in ways that lead them to believe they have infinite resources. That couldn't be farther from the truth.

Programmers too often think the platforms they are developing for have enough power for everything they do with the program, but they forget that not only that is wrong, but that the product they're developing will most likely be sharing those limited resources with other processes. If you take a close look, you'll notice that the ability of software to waste resources has been growing faster than the hardware industry has been able to produce more powerful equipment.

Programming twenty years ago was done trying to make the best of it with an old Amstrad with an 8086 CPU, 512KB of RAM and 20MB of hard disk space. That seems ridiculous by today's standards for most programmers, since most of them develop for fully equipped personal computers. But for some others it is not. Developers for embedded systems still have to work with hardware platforms with restrictions not much different from those. The fastest microprocessor in the auto industry, at the time of this writing, runs at 128MHz and sports a whooping 3MB of flash memory. Such capacities are a fraction of a regular contemporaneous PC, yet, they manage to be enough to control and monitor the systems on which we, today, rely to be safe while on the road.

Programmers from those times, would have a rather abrupt start with programming. They would begin almost immediately with Assembly and compiler internals. That would give them a very intimate perspective on how things were done at their lowest level. Because of such, in time, they would, somewhat *automagically*, tune their ability to generate code to produce it as optimized as they could, from what they knew. That type of introduction was the opposite to what today's programming students get. Most of you start with higher level languages, like

C# (if you're lucky) or Java (otherwise) and, then, possibly tryout lower levels and closer proximity to the hardware. It has been speculated that such teaching methodology is largely responsible for the quality decay of new programmers when compared to previous generations. Long discussions about this subject have been taken to some prominent computer-science related sites and discussion boards. It really is in your best interest to produce code as optimized as possible. Be the best you can be and make a difference by being able to deploy a product that not only does what it is supposed to, but also, does it well and efficiently. Not everyone can do so but you couldn't expect anything else from yourself than being able to exceed your own goals.

The optimizations a compiler is able to automate vary a lot from compiler to compiler. When it comes to optimizations, compilers are a double edged sword. They can be so smart for some things and so dumb for many others. So, let's help the compiler a little, by taking some work off its hands. It is not feasible to list here all possible code optimizations you could apply, but you'll be able to explore some of the most blatant ones.

6.1 Explicit Major Optimizations

The following optimizations are based in major changes to algorithms, by introducing new features and additional complexity. There are many variations of them, that can be applied and adapted to each case, but the basic theory is what you need to understand the most, so that you actually have a clue on what you need to do.

6.1.1 Caching

Caching is a method of transparently storing, in an area of easy access, data which will predictably be used frequently. The purpose of this optimization is to allow that piece of data to be served faster. They are usually small areas of storage. There are both software and hardware based caches that are implemented according to the usage. CPUs, hard drives and even many software elements do this to improve performance. They are frequently paired with choice optimization algorithms so that the most frequently accessed elements are the ones that stay in the cache. It is also common practice to simplify those algorithms by replacing them with algorithms that choose not the most accessed ones, but the most recently accessed. LRU, which stands for Least Recently Used, is one such scheme that removes from the current cache pool the element that seen the longer timespan since it was last used. The algorithm to use greatly depends on the situation and on the available information. Of course, this only pays off if the number of cache hits (accessing an element already in cache) is substantially greater than the number of cache misses (accessing an element that is not in cache, which must be loaded from a lower performance source – the backstore - and replace an element stored in the cache). Cache improvements are typically more notorious for reading data, than for writing it. The reason for that is that, in the case of a cache hit, reading does completely away with accessing the original, lower performance source, while writing implies that you have to eventually write the data back to its source. However, even in those cases, there are different policies that can be applied. Unsurprisingly, each one has its own drawbacks and there are

compromises between performance and integrity. These are:
- Write-through: this policy forces the synchronized writing of the data to both the cache and the backstore. Ensures data-integrity, but fails to offer any writing optimization.
- Write-back: when this policy is applied, the data is only written to the backstore when that element is cached-out (removed from cache) or when the system requests for a cache-flush (purging elements from the cache and writing the elements that were changed). The advantage of this method is that if there are several writes to the same element, only the final value is written, thus only accessing the backstore once for that element (unless, of course, the element is, for some reason, cached-out and cached-in again).
- Write-no-allocate: if this policy is applied, writes are never applied to the cache, unless the element is already there due to a cache-miss from a read. This means that, in the event that the element is not present in the cache, writing will be done directly to the backstore with no cache alterations.

6.1.2 Buffering

Buffering is similar to caching, although with some twists. While caching focuses on providing a continuous and random pool of the most used elements, buffering focuses on providing a pool of elements that are predictable to be accessed based on sequence. In other words, buffering is the method of, while obtaining a certain data element, also loading a set of subsequent elements since, due to the nature of the work to be done with those elements, it is highly likely that they will also be used. These algorithms are usually applied to loading data from disk drives. Because the performance of disk drives depends not only on the read speed, but also on the seek time (the period of time required to position the disk head on the right position), applying a buffer and reading a substantial amount of data greatly improves performance by reducing the amount of times that a seek needs to be performed.

6.1.3 Lazy evaluation and pro-activity

Lazy evaluation is the method of delaying the execution of a particular piece of code until its result is actually needed. The execution of a program depends on its input and the path it takes is always unpredictable. It is usual that you need the same value more than once, so it would be smart to store that value in some sort of a cache system. However, if, for some reason, that value ends up never being needed in the program, computing it becomes unnecessary. A smart way to deal with this is to only compute it when it is first needed.

On the other hand, you may need to do just the opposite in some situations. You'll be, sometimes, faced with situations where some of the computations are intensive and doing them *in situ* is computationally expensive because of the number of times they need to be repeated. On those situations you'll want to pro-actively pre-compute some values and store them.

In the end, if the value is going to be needed more than once, you can either apply lazy evaluation or pro-active evaluation and store the values in some sort of cache so it can be used whenever necessary. This way you avoid wasting precious cycles doing nothing useful or repeating the calculation of already determined values.

6.1.4 Data structure optimizations

Data structures are just like any other algorithm. They are usually complex in the implementation and the theory, but simple in the usage and the concept. Therefore, like any other algorithm, they are also susceptible to optimizations to their layout and the access methods.

6.1.4.1 Linked lists

The concept of locality of reference will be explained in more detail in section 6.2.2. However, a quick reference is in order now, when talking about data structure algorithms. Linked lists are, generally, traversed using an iterator. And that is an efficient and simple way to do it. There are, nevertheless, some vector implementations based on linked lists. They are, basically, linked lists that allow to refer directly (or so it seems) to the elements they contain. They frequently provide an overridden index/array subscript operator ("**operator[]**"). As you should know, to access any element in a list, you need to percolate every single element until you find the one you want. Lists have O(N) complexity. So, if you are going to use an overloaded "**operator[]**", for any usage of it, your code will have to travel through all the elements until it reaches the desired one. However, there are optimizations you can introduce. Suppose you have something like this:

```
1  template class<T> CMyListVectorElement
2  {
3      protected:
```

```
4       T m_element;
5       CmyListVectorElement<T> * m_prev,
6                               * m_next;
7       // here would be any other members or methods
8   };
9
10  template class<T> CMyListVector
11  {
12      protected:
13      CmyListVectorElement<T> * m_first,
14                              * m_last;
15
16      int m_count;
17
18      public:
19      // your subscript operator
20      T * operator[](int p_index);
21
22      // an imaginary operator to add elements
23      T * operator+=(T & p_element);
24
25      // here would be any other members or methods
26  };
```

Assume the linked list class always maintains a real-time count of the elements it holds, as most implementations do, and that our linked list is doubly linked. Therefore, you can, at any time, know the number of elements and get a pointer to the first and the last elements on the list. Now you introduce another two members to your list implementation, or to the vector implementation that encapsulates the list. An index and an element pointer, like this:

```
1   template class<T> CMyListVector
2   {
```

```
3      protected:
4        CMyListVectorElement<T> * m_first,
5                                * m_last,
6                                * m_current;
7
8        int m_count,       // number of elements
9            m_idxCurrent;  // last element
10
11
12     public:
13       // your subscript operator
14       T * operator[](int p_index);
15
16       // an imaginary operator to add elements
17       T * operator+=(T & p_element);
18
19     // here would be any other members or methods
20   };
```

It is predictable that when using arrays, the probability of using adjacent or close elements is high. Therefore, "**m_current**" and "**m_idxCurrent**" were added. Whenever one item is accessed, those members are updated to reflect which element was the last to be touched. And any new accesses using the indexing operator will need to consider those members. How? You have three pivot positions to evaluate: the first element in the list, the last element in the list and the last element to have been accessed. All of them have their indexes: 0, "**m_count - 1**" and "**m_idxCurrrent**". Therefore, by checking which pivot element has the smaller index difference to the element you want to access, you know from where to start counting to find the element you want to reach. By doing this, you are optimizing your accesses. Of course, there is one important thing you need to pay attention to: if you insert or remove elements, the new members must also reflect such changes. And if the element removed happens to be the one the "current" members point to, you have three choices. You either update them to point to the next element, or, depending on the distance, you update them to point either to the first or to the last elements in the list. An alternative solution that can be used in conjunction with the presented suggestion, is to apply the "divide and conquer" methodology. Instead of keeping only the "current", "first" and "last" pointers, you'd also keep the pointer to the middle element and perform the necessary simple calculations to determine where to count from. It would add only a short amount of complexity to your class but you'd get huge benefits in performance.

6.1.4.2 *Matrix abstraction classes*

A developer is often faced with a situation that requires him to write a class set to abstract the concept of a multidimensional matrix. It seems logical to use an overload of the index operator ("`operator[]`"). It is also common for that operator to return a reference to some sort of an array-type object, based on a class that also has the index operator properly overloaded. Well, this works, but may not be the best solution. You know, the index operator can have only one parameter. And it means that, for each dimension you need in that matrix, you'll need to add a new level of indirection. From a vector of elements, you'll have a vector of vectors of elements. And so on. Or, you could use the one operator that has an unlimited number of parameters: "`operator()`". By using this operator you can make it to have as many dimensions as you want and, more than that, you can optimize the guts of your class to take advantage of several of the optimization techniques described in this chapter.

6.2 Detail optimizations

Detail optimizations are based on small improvements to the code, organizing the data and the algorithms without subverting the functionality and without introducing major code changes.

6.2.1 Data based optimizations

The way you organize your data also plays an important role in optimizing your software. And, depending on the goals of your project, you may either want to save memory space, have the software faster or both. As always, a lot of optimizations are a trade-off between speed and size, but many others allow you to optimize both aspects at the same time.

6.2.1.1 Data bundling

Data bundling refers to the optimization technique of, in a single operation, dealing with an entire block of data, instead of a single element. By doing so, you are optimizing your memory accesses by using the maximum of your system's bus or register size. If you need, for example, to fill a block of memory with zeros, instead of going byte by byte, the best way to do it is by aligning it with the system bus width. Today's system buses can be of any size (most likely a byte multiple of a power of two). If you're running under a 32 bit architecture, your bus will most likely be either 32 bit or a power of two that is also a multiple of 32. Therefore, your bus width may be 32, 64, 128, and so on. So, when dealing with memory, unless your algorithm prevents it, you should prefer to move as much data as possible in one single operation, in order to reduce the amount of operations needed.

6.2.1.2 Data alignment

Another important optimization that is worth noting is data alignment. As much as possible, you should try to align your data in memory to a multiple of your target system's bus or register size. If your data is not aligned, you will incur in performance penalties due to the need of the CPU to align the data after loading it. Even if the data you're trying to access is the same size of the register, you're forcing the system to perform more than one operation to load your data, and more than one memory access. This is because even though the data block isn't aligned, the accesses are always aligned, which implies the system has to load each piece of the data, shift it into the right position and repeat this operation as many times as needed until the loading of that single element is complete.

6.2.1.3 Data packing

If you are at liberty to define your data structures and interested in saving memory space, packing data is one way you can achieve such goal. Usually, the compiler will place elements within structures to be aligned to the native word size of the target CPU. This means that, for example, in a 32 bit platform, a character, even though only 8 bits are useful, may occupy an entire 32 bit word. If you're developing for an embedded system, which usually has much tighter limits on memory, it's in your best interest to reduce wasted space as much as possible. The same happens if you're designing a network protocol. It is important to reduce traffic as much as possible, because bandwidth is expensive and carriers impose limits on the transfer amounts or charge by those amounts. So, you can, and in a lot of situations, should, pack your data together. It is easy to do so by using special directives available from the preprocessor. The directive in question is the "`#pragma pack(push, x)`" / "`#pragma pack(pop)`". The "x" allows you to select an alignment value. Typical useful values are powers of two. It is undetermined if any compiler at all will allow you any other values than powers of two. The reason to use a stack-based approach to this is that a lot of different alignment choices for structures can be needed in a project. Using a stack based approach to this allows to restore the previous context after declaring the structure. Take the following example:

```
1  ...
2  // previous stuff
3  ...
4  #pragma pack(push, 2)
5  ...
6  // some other stuff
7  ...
8  #pragma pack(push, 1)
9
10 typedef struct
11 {
12   char m_firstchar, m_secondchar;
13   unsigned short int m_onlyint;
14
15 } TMyType;
16
17 #pragma pack(pop)
18 ...
19 // yet some more stuff
```

```
20 ...
21 #pragma pack(pop)
22 ...
23 // ditto
24 ...
```

Here you can find two packing directives, in lines 4 and 8. However, nothing forbids the project to have other directives before or after. While you may want your "**TMyType**" structure to have an alignment at one byte, you do not want to disturb previous or subsequent code. Hence, the usage of a stack based approach. In this example, an instance of the "**TMyType**" structure will occupy exactly four bytes, because of the alignment defined in line 8. Should that alignment be changed to other values, the size of the structure might be different, depending on the compiler optimizations you chose and the decisions it makes.

6.2.1.4 Common subexpression elimination

This particular optimization method is based on the compiler finding instances of identical subexpressions, generally within a certain neighborhood of the first appearance of such expression and replacing it in the generated code by a variable still holding the calculation done. For example, the following code:

```
1  z = y * x + t;
2  w = y * x + r;
```

Could become the following:

```
1   tmp = y * x;
2   z = tmp + t;
3   w = tmp * r;
```

The actual benefits of such substitution greatly depend on the complexity of the expression computation-wise and, because of that, the compiler must evaluate the complexity of those expressions and decide whether to apply such optimization or not.

6.2.1.5 Constant propagation

All compilers, nowadays, evaluate expressions with constant values at compile time and replace them in-line with their actual values. This is probably the simplest optimization of all. An expression such as "`z = 65536 / 256;`" would not be stored as a store operation and a division, but directly as a referable value which, in this case, is 256.

6.2.2 Loop Optimizations

Loops are one of the constructs most susceptible to optimizations due to the overhead resulting from the instructions needed to control them. Because of their nature, that overhead is multiplied by as many times as they run. Worse still, a great deal of algorithms depend on loops chained inside one another, which means such overhead is exponentially increased. Reducing the need to run loops or the amount of cycles in each of them, is one way to do it but there are many other tricks to improve loop performance.

6.2.2.1 Array Iterations

While you are iterating over an array, in other languages where you cannot use pointers to directly refer to the elements of an array, you are forced to use the index of the elements you want to access. Basically you do this: `array[index]`. However, C++ allows you to use pointers to directly refer to the elements of the array. Using pointers, instead of indexing to iterate over the elements of an array, will give you a performance advantage, since using pointers means you only have to increment the pointer to refer to the next element or decrement it to refer to the previous. Every single CPU can perform increments or additions in one single instruction. On the other hand, using the index to refer to the element implies that the code hast first to multiply the index by the size of the elements and then add to it the base address of the array. And not many processors can do one instruction index calculations.

Assume "`array`" is an array of integers. You have:

```
for( int i = 0; i < _M_MAX; ++ i) array[i] = 0;
```

But you're better off doing this:

```
1  int * pa = array;
2  for( int i = 0; i < _M_MAX; ++i , ++ pa) *pa = 0;
```

However, for the sake of readability, most of the other examples displayed here will still use indexing.

6.2.2.2 Loop invariant code motion

Be sure to pay particular attention to this one. Often one does not realize that code being placed inside a loop could actually be placed outside, with minimal or no actual changes to that particular piece of code and without changing how the program works. By placing such code outside, you are ensuring those instructions run only once, saving the computer from having to waste time running such code as many times as cycles that loop is supposed to run. Take the following code as an example:

```
for(i = 0; i < _M_MAX_I; ++ i)
{
  a = b * c;
  z += 10 * (a + i);
}
```

As you can see, the value of the variable "z" depends on the value of variables "a" and "i". But the value of variable "a" is being calculated every time the program enters that cycle. If that cycle runs a thousand times, the value of "a" will be calculated a thousand times. But, unless "b" and "c" are volatile variables – which, for the matter of this discussion, it is assumed they're not – there is no point in repeatedly computing a value based on variables that remain unchanged. Therefore, the following code would be more appropriate:

```
a = b * c;

for(i = 0; i < _M_MAX_I; ++ i)
{
```

```
5      z += 10 * (a + i);
6    }
```

Also, a special case should get your attention. This case applies when you have variable declarations and chained cycles. Pay attention to the following example:

```
1   for(int i = 0; i < _M_MAX_I; ++ i)
2   {
3     for(int j = 0; j < _M_MAX_J; ++ j)
4     {
5       for(int k = 0; k < _M_MAX_K; ++ k)
6       {
7         z += _M_MAX_I * _M_MAX_J * i +
8              _M_MAX_J * j + k;
9       }
10    }
11  }
```

Here, you are declaring the variables "`i`", "`j`" and "`k`". Variable "`j`" is declared inside the "i-cycle" and the variable `k` is declared inside the "j-cycle". This means that "`j`" is going to be allocated and freed "`_M_MAX_I`" times, and "`k`" will be allocated and freed "`_M_MAX_I` * `_M_MAX_J`" times. If "`_M_MAX_I`" is, let's say, 1000, and "`_M_MAX_J`" is also 1000, then `j` will be allocated and freed 1000 times and "`k`" will be allocated and freed 1000000 times. This means 2002000 more operations on the stack than necessary (1001000 allocations and 1001000 releases). Therefore, the following would be a reasonable way to do it:

```
1   int i = 0, j = 0, k = 0;
2
3   for(i = 0; i < _M_MAX_I; ++ i)
4   {
5     for(j = 0; j < _M_MAX_J; ++ j)
6     {
7       for(k = 0; k < _M_MAX_K; ++ k)
8       {
9         z += _M_MAX_I * _M_MAX_J * i +
10             _M_MAX_J * j + k;
11      }
12    }
13  }
```

This way, you would be sure you would only create the variables once, and you would still initialize them at the beginning of each cycle, as you're supposed to. Remember, C and C++ do not initialize variables for you. You need to do it manually. And, with this, stack thrashing is gone.

6.2.2.3 Loop interchange

Loop interchange is related to a concept called locality of reference which, in turn, is strongly related to caching theory. Caching is not limited to the processor, since, for some programs, caching algorithms also have to be implemented in order for that program to deal more efficiently with input and output. Although the practical aspects my differ, the theory is just about the same. As you surely understand, CPU cache misses occur when your program attempts to access data that was not currently on cache. That forces the CPU to load a new block of data into the cache which, in the best case, will end up in free cache space and on the worst case, will force the CPU to flush out the block of data that has been accessed least recently.

It is, therefore, your goal to have your product generating the least possible count of cache misses. To be able to deliver the best possible performance, you need to have your program use the data in the cache as much as possible. You will find many such algorithms aimed at helping you take the best possible advantage from the CPU cache.

Applying loop interchange is very simple. Basically, you ensure that the order of variables in the chained cycles is such that you restrict each memory access in a loop on your program to a location as close as possible to the previous access. It's the case with loops dealing with a single matrix (to be seen further in why it may not be the case with loops that deal with more than one matrix). In C and C++, elements of the same row are stored contiguously. If you have a bi-dimensional array "**foo[rows, cols]**", the layout of the elements in memory will be "**foo[0, 0]**", "**foo[0, 1]**", "**foo[0, 2]**" and so on. This means that the best way to access the array elements in the array to make the most of the caching features of the machine is to access them one row at a time, like this:

```
int i = 0, int j = 0;

for(i = 0; i < rows; ++ i)
{
   for(j = 0; j < cols; ++ i)
   {
      foo[i, j] = i + j;
   }
}
```

It was mentioned earlier that it might not get you anywhere if you are accessing more than one matrix. This is because of the locality of reference. Different matrices may have been placed in positions such that they do not end up both in cache at the same time. With today's cache sizes in regular personal computers, that effect may be attenuated or even eliminated. However, the same may not be the case for other types of platforms, especially embedded systems. And make sure you can, when appropriate, interchange loops without subverting your algorithm.

6.2.2.4 Loop fusion

Where cache misses either aren't a problem or are a smaller problem than having two loops similarly dimensioned running consecutively, joining two loops together can bring you some performance by reducing the overhead resulting from the loop control instructions and jumps, as well as reducing code size. The following is a trivial example:

```
1   int i,
2       a[_M_MAX],
3       b[_M_MAX];
4
5   for (i = 0; i < _M_MAX; ++ i) a[i] = 'a';
6   for (i = 0; i < _M_MAX; ++ i) b[i] = 'b';
```

The loops can be merged together in the following way:

```
1   int i,
2       a[_M_MAX],
3       b[_M_MAX];
4
5   for (i = 0; i < _M_MAX; ++ i)
6   {
```

```
7      a[i] = 'a';
8      b[i] = 'b';
9  }
```

Be aware that, due to the previously explained concept of locality of reference, this technique may not always be the best option. In some cases the opposite technique, "Loop Fission", presented below, may be a more suitable option.

6.2.2.5 Loop fission

Loop fission is the opposite to the loop fusion method. Instead of trying to reduce overhead from loop control instructions, loop fission attempts to make a better use of locality of reference, by splitting, in different loops, accesses to separate memory areas. The exact opposite transformation operation from loop fusion occurs:

```
1  int i,
2      a[_M_MAX],
3      b[_M_MAX];
4
5  for (i = 0; i < _M_MAX; ++ i)
6  {
7      a[i] = 'a';
8      b[i] = 'b';
9  }
```

Then becomes:

```
1  int i,
2      a[_M_MAX],
```

```
3        b[_M_MAX];
4
5    for (i = 0; i < _M_MAX; ++ i) a[i] = 'a';
6    for (i = 0; i < _M_MAX; ++ i) b[i] = 'b';
```

This transformation brings additional benefits in some multi-core or multi-threaded systems able to split a single task between multiple execution paths.

6.2.2.6 Loop reversal

By applying this optimization, the order in which the loop is run gets reversed. This not only reduces code size, but also reduces variable (and thus, register) allocation. Consider an example of a function whose objective is to add the values of all the elements in an array. The parameters of the function are the array and the number of elements in it. Typically, you'd write something like this:

```
1    int sum_elements(int * p_array, int p_count)
2    {
3      int l_sum = 0;
4
5      for(int l_itr = 0; l_itr < p_count; ++ l_itr)
6        l_sum += p_array[l_itr];
7
8      return(l_sum);
9    }
```

As you can see, you're creating two new variables in the stack. More importantly, in other situations not as trivial as this example, such variables may be dependencies. One of them is unnecessary. By eliminating it and using a decrement loop instead of an increment loop, you eliminate the dependencies allowing other forms of optimization. Take a look at a first stage optimization of the previous example:

```
1   int sum_elements(int * p_array, int p_count)
2   {
3     int l_sum = 0;
4     -- p_count;
5
6     for(; p_count >= 0; -- p_count)
7       l_sum += p_array[p_count];
8
9     return(l_sum);
10  }
```

This example works because "**p_count**" is passed by copy to the function and, therefore, can be discarded if no other operations inside the function depend on its value. And the function can be further optimized by removing the array indexing, because although the array is passed by pointer, the pointer to the array is passed by value, rendering it disposable:

```
1   int sum_elements(int * p_array, int p_count)
2   {
3     int l_sum = 0;
4
5     for(; p_count > 0; -- p_count, -- p_array)
6       l_sum += *p_array;
7
8     return(l_sum);
9   }
```

And the code just got a lot less complicated for you, the

compiler and the CPU.

6.2.2.7 Loop unrolling

Loop unrolling, also known as loop unwinding, is a technique for optimization that sacrifices the binary size of the program to improve execution speed by minimizing penalties resulting from branching, pointer arithmetic, index management and everything else related to controlling the loop. This works by reducing the number of cycles in a loop by repeating the instructions within a single cycle. In the end, the number of cycles will be reduced to "N/m" where "N" is the number of cycles required by the algorithm and "m" is the number of repetitions. Of course that, if "N" is not divisible by "m", then the remainder of operations needed would have to be done outside the loop. So, consider the following example:

```
1  char array[_M_MAX];
2
3  for(int i = 0; i < _M_MAX; ++ i) array[i] = 0;
```

Assuming "**_M_MAX**" is divisible by 2, such code could be optimized by doing this:

```
1  char array[_M_MAX];
2
3  for(int i = 0; i < _M_MAX / 2; ++ i)
4  {
5    array[i * 2] = 0;
6    array[i * 2 + 1] = 0;
7  }
```

And if you've paid attention to the previous sections, such code could be further optimized this way:

```
1   char array[_M_MAX];
2   char *pa = array;
3
4   for(int i = 0; i < _M_MAX / 2; ++ i, ++ pa)
5   {
6     *pa = 0;
7     ++ pa;
8     *pa = 0;
9   }
```

But it's not all. Take a look at the same code now. Assume, just for the sake of the argument, that the code is divisible by 8 and that "**DWORD**" has been defined as being a 4 byte unsigned integer:

```
1   char array[_M_MAX];
2   DWORD * pa = (DWORD *) array;
3
4   for(int i = 0; i < _M_MAX / 8; ++ i, ++ pa)
5   {
6     *pa = 0;
7     ++ pa;
8     *pa = 0;
9   }
```

As you can see, you're not only unrolling the loop, you're also bundling the data. For string and memory operations, for example, this is a very common and efficient optimization. This is a simplified version of a potential memory block cleaning algorithm. Loop unwinding comes with many advantages but, as with almost all optimization algorithms, it is not free of disadvantages. It improves the code by reducing branch penalties (the cost of having the processor jumping between instructions, namely, jumping from the end of the loop to the beginning after completion of each cycle), the possibility of parallel execution of the statements within the cycle (if, of course, they are independent of each other), and the possibility of a dynamic implementation, should the number of cycles be unknown at compile time. On the other hand, it increases the binary code size (which may be undesirable for any kind of application that requires a low memory footprint and implies an increase in instruction cache misses), code readability may be reduced (this can be prevented if the compiler performs the optimization automatically at compile time), and an increase in register allocation (which may result in decreased performance).

6.2.2.8 Loop unswitching

Loop unswitching works by duplication of a loop's body, moving a conditional existing inside the loop to the outside of it. It is a special case of loop invariant code motion. Take the following example:

```
1  int i, j, a[_M_MAX], b[_M_MAX];
2
3  // do something with j along the way
4
5  for(i = 0; i < _M_MAX; ++ i)
6  {
7      a[i] *= 2;
8      if(j) b[i] = 0;
9  }
```

Such could be re-written the following way:

```
1  int i, j, a[_M_MAX], b[_M_MAX];
2
3  // do something with j along the way
4  if(j)
5  {
6    for(i = 0; i < _M_MAX; ++ i)
7    {
8      a[i] *= 2;
9      b[i] = 0;
10   }
11 }
12 else
13 {
14   for(i = 0; i < _M_MAX; ++ i)
15   {
16     a[i] *= 2;
17   }
18 }
```

By splitting the loop this way, you're ensuring the comparison only takes place once. This increases code size, but decreases the overhead from a repeated comparison. As said before, sometimes optimizations are trade-offs between speed and code size.

7 Final notes

As you could see from all the topics I presented in this book, there is plenty of potential for you to improve your skills and the quality of your code. A lot of what I presented depends greatly on one thing: discipline. This is your most important ally. Without it, there will be no amount of tools or tricks that will save you. The quality of the code can be improved in several aspects. You can improve it in terms of safety, security, reliability and performance. However, this is not the ending, it is just the beginning, as this manual is just an introduction.

Future editions will contain much more information and topics for you to explore and the subjects related with applying appropriate practices when developing software are extensive and may very well justify a sequel.

You need to always remember that science, and especially computer science, is always evolving. You need to keep yourself up to date with evolution and the new technologies. And you should always try to improve yourself. I'd like to wish you the best success possible, and I hope that this book has met and, if possible, exceeded your best expectations.

So, as a final advice, don't settle for just what was discussed in this manual, instead try to learn more and do some research. Don't let yourself be bound by the legacy of the past. Think ahead and outside of the box. Develop for the future, embrace your resources and all the possibilities and you'll end up with great products with very high quality. There's no greater advantage. Except, perhaps, a good marketing team.

Good luck and best regards.

www.ingramcontent.com/pod-product-compliance
Lightning Source LLC
Chambersburg PA
CBHW071425170526
45165CB00001B/394